Cross Ties

Cross Ties

Selected Poems

X. J. KENNEDY

The University of Georgia Press
Athens

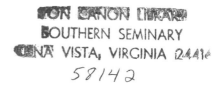

© 1985 by X. J. Kennedy
Published by the University of Georgia Press
Athens, Georgia 30602

All rights reserved
Set in 9 on 12 Linotron 202 Palatino

The paper in this book meets the guidelines for
permanence and durability of the Committee on
Production Guidelines for Book Longevity of the
Council on Library Resources.

Printed in the United States of America
89 88 87 86 85   5 4 3 2 1

Library of Congress Cataloging in Publication Data

Kennedy, X. J.
    Cross ties.

    I. Title.
PS3521.E563A6   1985   811'.54   84-8679
ISBN 0-8203-0737-8
ISBN 0-8203-0738-6 (pbk.)

FOR DOROTHY

The publication of this book is supported by a grant from the National Endowment for the Arts, a federal agency.

Acknowledgments

The author thanks the publishers of the following books and chapbooks, from which some of the work in this selection has been drawn: *Nude Descending a Staircase* (1961) and *Growing into Love* (1969), published by Doubleday & Company; *Bulsh* (1970), published by Burning Deck; *Breaking and Entering* (1971), published by Oxford University Press; *Emily Dickinson in Southern California* (1974) and *Did Adam Name the Vinegarroon?* (1982), published by David R. Godine; *Celebrations after the Death of John Brennan* (1974), published by Penmaen Press; *One Winter Night in August* (1975), *The Phantom Ice Cream Man* (1979), and *The Forgetful Wishing Well* (1985), published by Margaret K. McElderry Books and Atheneum; *Three Tenors, One Vehicle* (with James Camp and Keith Waldrop, 1975), published by Open Places; *French Leave: Translations* (1983), published by Robert L. Barth; *Hangover Mass* (1984), published by Bits Press.

For previously publishing poems now first collected, he thanks the editors of *The Atlantic, Bits, Boston Jewish Advocate, Boston Review, Canto, Carolina Quarterly, Cricket: The Magazine for Children, Cumberland Poetry Review, Field, Hampton-Sydney Poetry Review, Harper's, Harvard Magazine, Inquiry, Jam To-Day, Kentucky Poetry Review, Limberlost Review, Massachusetts Review, New Boston Review, New Statesman, Occurrence, Open Places, Paris Review, Parnassus: Poetry in Review, Ploughshares, Poetry, Poetry NOW, Seneca Review, Southern Poetry Review, Sou'wester, Times Literary Supplement, Tri-Quarterly, West Hills Review, Wittenberg Review;* and Robert Wallace, editor of the anthology *Light Year '84* (Bits Press). "Flitting Flies" was first published as a broadside by the Chimera Press; "Dirty English Potatoes," as a broadside by the Folger Shakespeare Library. "No Neutral Stone" was written in 1977 for the Phi Beta Kappa Society of Brown University.

The work of many editors over the years is reflected in the texts of some of these poems. The author thanks them all, especially Naomi Burton, Peter Davison, Donald Hall, Margaret K. McElderry, Howard Moss, John Frederick Nims, Sarah Saint-Onge, Jan Schreiber, and Jon Stallworthy.

Contents

I. 1956–1961

Intermission: Songs

II. 1962–1968

Intermission: Light Verse

III. 1969–1971

Intermission: Epigrams & Epitaphs

IV. 1972–1977

Intermission: For Children

V. 1978–1984

I

1956–1961

On a Child Who Lived One Minute

Into a world where children shriek like suns
Sundered from other suns on their arrival,
She stared, and saw the waiting shape of evil,
But couldn't take its meaning in at once,
So fresh her understanding, and so fragile.

Her first breath drew a fragrance from the air
And put it back. However hard her agile
Heart danced, however full the surgeon's satchel
Of healing stuff, a blackness tiptoed in her
And snuffed the only candle of her castle.

Oh, let us do away with elegiac
Drivel! Who can restore a thing so brittle,
So new in any jingle? Still I marvel
That, making light of mountainloads of logic,
So much could stay a moment in so little.

Faces from a Bestiary

Suggested by the twelfth-century
Livre des Créatures of Philip de Thaun

1

The Lion sleeps with open eyes
That none may take him by surprise.
The Son of God he signifies.

For when a Lion stillborn lies
His mother circles him and cries.
Then on the third day he will rise.

2

Hyena is a beast to hate.
No man hath seen him copulate.
He is unto himself a mate.

You who this creature emulate,
Who with your mirrors fornicate,
Do not repent. It is too late.

Nude Descending a Staircase

Toe upon toe, a snowing flesh,
A gold of lemon, root and rind,
She sifts in sunlight down the stairs
With nothing on. Nor on her mind.

We spy beneath the banister
A constant thresh of thigh on thigh—
Her lips imprint the swinging air
That parts to let her parts go by.

One-woman waterfall, she wears
Her slow descent like a long cape
And pausing, on the final stair
Collects her motions into shape.

Solitary Confinement

She might have stolen from his arms
Except that there was nothing left
To steal. There was the crucifix
Of silver good enough to hock
But how far could she go on it
And what had he left her to pack
And steal away with and lay down
By someone new in a new town?

She put the notion back
And turned her look up where the clock,
Green ghost, swept round its tethered hand
That had made off with many nights
But no more could break from its shelf
Than she could quit this bed where breath
By breath these years he'd nailed her fast
Between two thieves, him and herself.

Little Elegy

for a child who skipped rope

Here lies resting, out of breath,
Out of turns, Elizabeth
Whose quicksilver toes not quite
Cleared the whirring edge of night.

Earth whose circles round us skim
Till they catch the lightest limb,
Shelter now Elizabeth
And for her sake trip up Death.

First Confession

Blood thudded in my ears. I scuffed,
   Steps stubborn, to the telltale booth
Beyond whose curtained portal coughed
   The robed repositor of truth.

The slat shot back. The universe
   Bowed down his cratered dome to hear
Enumerated my each curse,
   The sip snitched from my old man's beer,

My sloth pride envy lechery,
   The dime held back from Peter's Pence
With which I'd bribed my girl to pee
   That I might spy her instruments.

Hovering scale-pans when I'd done
   Settled their balance slow as silt
While in the restless dark I burned
   Bright as a brimstone in my guilt

Until as one feeds birds he doled
   Seven Our Fathers and a Hail
Which I to double-scrub my soul
   Intoned twice at the altar rail

Where Sunday in seraphic light
   I knelt, as full of grace as most,
And stuck my tongue out at the priest:
   A fresh roost for the Holy Ghost.

Inscriptions After Fact

for Frank Brownlow

LILITH

Adam's first wife had soft lips but no soul:
He looked her in the eye, back looked a hole.
Her small ear lay, a dry well so profound
No word he pebbled in it drew a sound.

Could he complete what God had left half-wrought?
He practiced in a looking lake, he taught
Stray rudiments of wriggle, where to stand
Her liltless feet. She handed him her hand.

Her breasts stood up but in them seemed to rise
No need for man. He roamed lone in her thighs
And inmost touching, most knew solitude:
In vacant rooms, on whom can one intrude?

O let down mercy on a poor man who clings
To echoes, beds him with imaginings!
Sweet Lord, he prayed, *with what shade do I lie?*
Second came she whom he begot us by.

THE SIRENS

Stayed in one place and did no work
But warble ditties a bit loose,
Strike poses, primp, bedeck their rock
With primrose boxes. Odysseus

Salt-lipped, long-bandied before winds,
Heard in his loins a bass chord stir,

Said to his men, "Men, stop your ears—
I need not, being an officer."

Under the deaf indifferent tread
Of wood on water, round each oar
Broke like the grapes of Ilium
Ripening clusters of blue air

And when those soft sounds stole, there grew
The notion as he champed his bit
That love was all there was, and death
Had something to be said for it.

Roared as the music sweetened, railed
Against his oarsmen's bent wet slopes,
Imprisoned in propriety
And pagan ethic. Also ropes.

Sails strummed. The keel drove tapestries
Of distance on the sea's silk-loom
Leaving those simple girls beyond
Woven undone rewoven foam

To wonder: had they lost their touch?
Unbroken yet, a woof of sea
Impelled him to his dying dog,
Pantoufles, and Penelope.

NARCISSUS SUITOR

He touched her face and gooseflesh crept—
He loved her as it were
Not for her look though it lay deep
But what he saw in her.

Drew her up wobbling in his arms,
Laid lips by her smooth cheek,
And would have joined the two of him
In one cohesive Greek

When soft by his obdurate ear
Like lips, two ripples pursed—
These syllables distinct and pure
Bubbled to air, and burst:

"Oh keep your big feet to yourself
Good sir, goddammit stop!
I'm not that sort of pool at all!
I'll scream! I'll call a cop!

"Settle me back in my right bed
Or you shall edge your skiff
Through ice as limber as your eyes,
As blue, as frozen stiff."

THEATER OF DIONYSUS
Athens, U.S. Sixth Fleet

By the aisle on a stone bench
In the Theater of Dionysus
I make a flock of Greek kids smile
Sketching them Mickey Mouses

Where beery Aristophanes
By sanction till night's fall
Ribbed Eleusinian mysteries
With queer-joke and pratt-fall.

On high from the sacked Parthenon
A blackbird faintly warbles.

Sellers of paperweights resell
The Elgin marbles.

Here where queen-betrayed
Agamemnon had to don
Wine-purple robes, boys in torn drabs
Try my whitehat on,

Over stones where Orestes fled
The sonorous Furies
Girls hawking flyspecked postcards
Pursue the tourist.

Here in her anguish-mask
Andromache
Mourned her slain son—"Young man,
Aren't you from Schenectady?"

As I trudge down, a pebble breaks
Rattling across stone tiers,
Scattering echoes: do I kick
A watcher's skull downstairs?

Silence imponders back
As I take the stage, the pebble
Stilled on a lower tier.
Trailing home now, the child rabble.

I stand in the center of the stage,
Could speak, but the sun's setting
In back of neon signs. Night unsheathes
Her chill blade. Better be getting

Back to the destroyer, radared bark,
No thresh of oars, sails with gods' crests—
Does the wind stir through the dark
Or does a throng of ghosts?

I run. Inaudible laughter drives
Offstage my spirit
As in the parched grass, wind routs
A white shiver before it.

B Negative

M/6o/5FT4/W PROT

You know it's April by the falling-off
In coughdrop boxes—fewer people cough—
    By daisies' first white eyeballs in the grass
And every dawn more underthings cast off.

Though plumtrees stretch recovered boughs to us
And doubledecked in green, the downtown bus,
    Love in one season—so your stab-pole tells—
Beds down, and buds, and is deciduous.

Now set down burlap bag. In pigeon talk
The wobbling pigeon flutes on the sidewalk,
    Struts on the breeze and clicks leisurely wings
As if the corn he ate grew on a stalk.

So plump he topples where he tries to stand,
He pecks my shoelaces, come to demand
    Another sack, another fifteen cents,
And yet—who else will eat out of my hand?

It used to be that when I laid my head
And body with it down by you in bed
    You did not turn from me nor fall to sleep
But turn to fall between my arms instead

And now I lay bifocals down. My feet
Forget the twist that brought me to your street.
    I can't make out your face for steamed-up glass
Nor quite call back your outline on the sheet.

I know how, bent to a movie magazine,
The hobo's head lights up, and from its screen

Imagined bosoms in slow motion bloom
And no director interrupts the scene:

I used to purchase in the Automat
A cup of soup and fan it with my hat
    Until a stern voice from the changebooth crashed
Like nickels: *Gentlemen do not do that.*

Spring has no household, no abiding heat,
Pokes forth no bud from branches of concrete,
    Nothing to touch you, nothing you can touch—
The snow, at least, keeps track of people's feet.

The springer spaniel and the buoyant hare
Seem half at home reclining in mid-air
    But Lord, the times I've leaped the way they do
And looked round for a foothold—in despair.

The subway a little cheaper than a room,
I browse the *News*—or so the guards assume—
    And there half-waking, tucked in funny sheets,
Hurtle within my mile-a-minute womb.

Down streets that wake up earlier than wheels
The routed spirit flees on dusty heels
    And in the soft fire of a muscatel
Sits up, puts forth its fingertips, and feels—

Down streets so deep the sun can't vault their walls,
Where one-night wives make periodic calls,
    Where cat steals stone where rat makes off with child
And lyre and lute lie down under three balls,

Down blocks in sequence, fact by separate fact,
The human integers add and subtract
    Till in a cubic room in some hotel
You wake one day to find yourself abstract

And turn a knob and hear a voice: *Insist*
On Jiffy Blades, they're tender to the wrist—
    Then static, then a squawk as though your hand
Had shut some human windpipe with a twist.

I know how, lurking under trees by dark,
Poor loony stranglers out to make their mark
    Reach forth shy hands to touch some woman's hair—
I pick up after them in Central Park.

Landscapes with Set-Screws

I
THE AUTUMN IN NORFOLK SHIPYARD

Is a secret one infers
From camouflage. Scrap steel
Betrays no color of season,
Corrosion works year-round.
But in sandblasted stubble
Lurks change: parched thistle burr,
Blown milkweed hull—dried potholes
After tides reassume their foam.

Destroyers mast to mast,
Mechanical conifers,
Bear pointed lights. Moored tankers
Redden slow as leaves.
Under the power crane
Dropped girders lie like twigs,
In drydock ripened tugs
Burst pod-wide—ringbolts bobble
To quiet upon steel-plate
Mud. A flake of paint falls,

Green seas spill last year's needles.

II
AIRPORT IN THE GRASS

Grasshopper copters whir,
Blue blurs
Traverse dry air,

Cicadas beam a whine

On which to zero in flights
Of turbojet termites,

A red ant carts
From the fusilage of the wren that crashed
Usable parts

And edging the landingstrip,
Heavier than air the river
The river
The rustbucket river
Revs up her motors forever.

Ladies Looking for Lice

after Rimbaud

When the child's forehead is afire with red
Tortures and he longs for vague white dreams to come,
Two enchantress big sisters steal close to his bed
With tinselly fingers, nails of platinum.

By a casement thrown open they sit the child down
Where blue air bathes stealthily the budded stalk
And in his locks thick with dew and along his crown
Their sorceress hands thin and terrible walk.

He traces the song of their hesitant breath,
Spumed honey that feels forth slow tendrils, the hiss
That now and then breaks it: spit blown through the teeth
And sucked back on the lips, or desire for a kiss.

He hears their black lashes beat through the perfume
Of the quiet and a crackle like static: the slice
Of their fingernails, queens of his indolent gloom,
Passing death sentences on little lice.

Now in him a wine mounts: Laziness,
Sound that can drive mad, a harmonica sigh,
And the child feels in time to each slow caress
Rush and recede endlessly the desire to cry.

One A.M. with Voices

Hers: What do you squander night for
       In coupling on a page
       Rhymes no man pronounces?—
       Is it love or rage?
       The crouched cat pounces dream-mice,
       True mice play blindman's buff.
       For God's sake give the thing a pitch,
       I've lain cold long enough.

His: Did I write rhymes for love, sweet mouse,
       Then I'd have taken instead
       A sheaf of verses to my thighs,
       And rage—that's rape indeed.
       You are the single love I have.
       Be still. A further rhyme
       Plays cat-and-mouse about my head—
       Just a few minutes. I'm
       A mouser that must hunt awake
       With a green eye that roams:
       A shivering candle I must bear
       Where shapes twitch in dark rooms.

Hers: More endless rooms, old creeping tom,
       Than light can overtake.
       When did you ever catch a mouse
       But lean ones, wide awake?
       The plump drop to the hunter
       Who gropes them out when blind—
       How can you keep an eye on
       Every mousehole of the mind?
       Put cat and light out. You shall have
       The warmed side of the bed
       That sleep may with a breath blow out
       This guttering in your head.

Intermission

SONGS

In a Prominent Bar in Secaucus One Day

To the tune of "The Old Orange Flute"
or the tune of "Sweet Betsy from Pike"

In a prominent bar in Secaucus one day
Rose a lady in skunk with a topheavy sway,
Raised a knobby red finger—all turned from their beer—
While with eyes bright as snowcrust she sang high and clear:

"Now who of you'd think from an eyeload of me
That I once was a lady as proud as could be?
Oh I'd never sit down by a tumbledown drunk
If it wasn't, my dears, for the high cost of junk.

"All the gents used to swear that the white of my calf
Beat the down of the swan by a length and a half.
In the kerchief of linen I caught to my nose
Ah, there never fell snot, but a little gold rose.

"I had seven gold teeth and a toothpick of gold,
My Virginia cheroot was a leaf of it rolled
And I'd light it each time with a thousand in cash—
Why the bums used to fight if I flicked them an ash.

"Once the toast of the Biltmore, the belle of the Taft,
I would drink bottle beer at the Drake, never draft,
And dine at the Astor on Salisbury steak
With a clean tablecloth for each bite I did take.

"In a car like the Roxy I'd roll to the track,
A steel-guitar trio, a bar in the back,
And the wheels made no noise, they turned over so fast,
Still it took you ten minutes to see me go past.

"When the horses bowed down to me that I might choose,
I bet on them all, for I hated to lose.

Now I'm saddled each night for my butter and eggs
And the broken threads race down the backs of my legs.

"Let you hold in mind, girls, that your beauty must pass
Like a lovely white clover that rusts with its grass.
Keep your bottoms off barstools and marry you young
Or be left—an old barrel with many a bung.

"For when time takes you out for a spin in his car
You'll be hard-pressed to stop him from going too far
And be left by the roadside, for all your good deeds,
Two toadstools for tits and a face full of weeds."

All the house raised a cheer, but the man at the bar
Made a phonecall and up pulled a red patrol car
And she blew us a kiss as they copped her away
From that prominent bar in Secaucus, N.J.

Barking Dog Blues

I hear those barking dog blues
Every getting-out-of-bed of day.
I hear those barking dog blues
Every getting-out-of-bed of day,
Barking dog blues
That chase my other blues away.

Mister Municipal Dog-Catcher
Won't you throw me in your pound?
Cause I just might bite somebody
If you leave me running round.

Baby, some men want to marry—
Me, I'd rather go to jail.
You drive me round in circles
Like a tin can tied to my tail.

Quit your messing round my little dog
Cause my big dog got a bone.
If you don't want my big dog
Leave my little dog alone.

Hear me barking Monday morning
In the driving rain.
I'll lay down in your kennel
But I won't wear your chain.

Lizabet's Song to the Senate
and the House of Representatives

Following the death of her
astronaut lover from meteor damage
(from a ballad,
"The Man in the Manmade Moon")

Coal black is the raven, coal black is the rook,
Coal black is the shark in the billow.
Where I once had a Bill to drive back my chill
There's a cold blackeyed pea on my pillow.

In my nightmare once more I stood at his door
Crying, "Love, let me in let me in,
For the winter winds rave in my permanent wave
And the raindrops dilute my sloe gin."

And the door it swung wide and hanging inside
At the height of the man I had lost
Was a featureless face full of outer space
On a neck like a rocket exhaust.

Song to the Tune of "Somebody Stole My Gal"

I'm fed up with people
who say, Boo hoo, somebody
stole my myths.
                W. D. Snodgrass

Somebody stole my myths,
Stole all their gists and piths.
Somebody pinched my Juno and Pan,
Crooked Dionysus
And caused my spiritual crisis.
Some no-good no-account
Made my centaur dismount.
Some bugger in a laboratory coat with test-tube in hand
Mixed nitrogen with glycerin and poof! went my promised
        land, oh,
Hear me crying,
Don't much like forever dying—
Somebody stole my myths.

Great Chain of Being

Drinking smooth wine in a castle or digging potatoes knee-deep in
    dung,
Everybody in creation knew just how high or how low he hung
On that ladder with Lord God at the top and dumb mud at the
    bottom rung,
                    Great Chain of Being,
                    Great Chain of Being.

Well, man was top dog on mother earth and woman was his
    marrow bone
And a woman giving suck to a child cut more ice than a woman
    alone
And the cruddiest of sparrows glittered more than any precious
    stone
                    In hierarchy,
                    In hierarchy.

Then Copernicus picked up his hammer, Galileo held the spike,
And they hit that Great Chain a wallop just as pretty as you like—
Old Earth went flying from her center like the sprocket out of a
    bike,
                    All its spokes busted,
                    All its spokes busted.

Well, nowadays, every creature goes rattling around, worked loose
    from that golden chain,
And the angleworm and the angel can't connect with each other
    again,
And me, I'm fixing to let myself play out in the pouring rain,
                    Snapped off and dangling,
                    Snapped off and dangling.

Now I wonder who's been sitting in the Good Lord's old arm chair,
I wonder if there's still snakes down below and a Blessed Mother
    up there
Keeping an eye on me, or just the credit bureau and Medicare—
                    Is *seeing believing?*
                    Is *seeing believing?*

Uncle Ool's Complaint
Against the Ill-Paid Life of Verse

In ancient Greece
Where men chased fleece
    And girls wore golden panties,
Bard Orpheus
Ran smack across
    A pack of crazed Bacchantes.
Torn limb from limb
They soon had him—
    By Christ, it was disarming!
For woman least
Of any beast
    Gives in to music's charming.

When Mother Church
Preened on her perch
    Above the Middle Ages,
No hunch-backed serf
That dredged his turf
    Dared strike for living wages.
On tap like malt,
Below the salt,
    The lean-eyed bard sat anchored
Biding his time
To bawl his rhyme
    Through tankard's clink on tankard.

Today some starve
Behind iron bars,
    Rage ravening their hearts,
Some die with gouts
As laureates
    Or commissars of arts.
But who'd sit late

And beat his pate
  Against stone walls of meter?
They are ill-paid
That ply that trade.
  I find hard drinking sweeter.

As dogs delight
To bark and bite
  And bees to drone an orchard,
Old oily whales
To thrash their tails
  And martyrs to be tortured,
At bar or booth
To tell the truth
  It is my solemn pleasure
While night grows late
To meditate
  On emptying a measure.

Our bones themselves
Lead stone-blind wolves
  On leashes three-score long,
Their seeing-eyes,
But they catch wise
  As, aging, we smell strong.
Brown beer! brown beer
To last all here
  Till the toothless dogs lap mush!
To die from rhyme
Or drink takes time—
  Sit down, now, what's your rush?

Flagellant's Song

When I was young
And jackass-hung,
  A lecher by persuasion,
Each girl who stirred
My nesting bird,
  I'd rise to her occasion,

But now that snow
Across my brow
  Has flittered down and perched,
I can't address
A girl unless
  My backside's smartly birched.

So whip away!
Flail, flog, and flay!
  Hooray! the birchbark's thwacking!
That whistling wood
Incites my mood,
  And soon I'm hot attacking.

When men grow old,
Desire grows mold
  And wives turn cold and thoughtful.
Then, tender words
Are for the birds!
  They'll give good wives a gutful.

Oh, flail and lash
Inspire men's flesh;
  Ripe oats and hay, race horses.
If more wives flayed

They'd be well laid,
  And rare would be divorces.

I dreamed a sight
Of Sade last night,
  Alive like you and me.
Your grace, said I,
How did you die?
  By little bits, said he.

Talking Dust Bowl

Old cow's almost dry now, her hooves scrape hard dirt.
Where's the man going to pay me what I'm worth?
Forty acres played out, soil like the corn meal low in the can,
Reminds me of a woman holding back on a man.
Nights, hot nights I walk by the warped board fence
Hoping to find a fresh water break-through or some sense.
Seeing my kids run round in washed-out flour bags
Makes my heart move like a man with one lame foot that drags.
Hearing my kids whine in the dark through their bunk room door,
We only had nine stew beans, can't we have some more?
Sending 'em to bed before sundown every night
So they won't run around and work up an appetite.
Had my fill of hanging around this town
Like a picture on a nail waiting to be took down.
Seen my name writ ten times on the same yellow pad,
Don't mean a damn, they don't send for you, makes a man mad.
Stalk of corn can grub its roots deep, find iron in dry ground.
Let a man try, he can't go deep—where's food to be found?
Shoes wearing thin not from plowing, not from working a road,
Just from tromping back and forth carrying their same old load.
Beth used to wear her hair in a neat combed braid,
Now she lets it fall any old way down her forehead.
Black topsoil used to roll off from the eye straight north,
Nothing now but wind towing dust clouds back and forth.
No more point in hanging around this town.
Going to fix me an old Ford, lay those patched tires round and
    round,
Going to head due west where the oranges hang low,
Let my kids pick too, eat red pears right off of the bough,
Furry peach bending the branch, and its stem thumb-thick,
Shrinking back from your hand like a young cunt from a prick.
Dust clouds bearing down now, dust stretching from pole to pole.
No use staying here till I'm dried in the long dust bowl.

At Brown Crane Pavilion

after Ts'ui Hao, about 800 A.D.

An old god-man rode off on his brown crane.
What's left behind? This dedicated shack.
Ten hundred years, white clouds have wandered by.
Brown crane's long gone. Not likely he'll be back.

By river glow, each leaf sticks out its veins.
Parrot Island grass—oh, smell it! shed your shoes!
Sun knows its way down home. Wish I knew mine.
Got the mist on the river, waves on the river blues.

II
1962–1968

Nothing in Heaven Functions As It Ought

Nothing in Heaven functions as it ought:
Peter's bifocals, blindly sat on, crack;
His gates lurch wide with the cackle of a cock,
Not turn with a hush of gold as Milton had thought;
Gangs of the slaughtered innocents keep huffing
The nimbus off the Venerable Bede
Like that of an old dandelion gone to seed;
And the beatific choir keep breaking up, coughing.

But Hell, sleek Hell hath no freewheeling part:
None takes his own sweet time, none quickens pace.
Ask anyone, *How come you here, poor heart?*—
And he will slot a quarter through his face,
You'll hear an instant click, a tear will start
Imprinted with an abstract of his case.

Artificer

Blessing his handiwork, his drawbridge closed,
  He sabbathed on a hill of hand-tooled wax.
On stainless steel chrysanthemums there posed
  Little gold bees with twist-keys in their backs.

Nothing could budge in this his country: lewd
  Leaves could go slither other people's hills.
His thrushes tried tin whistles in their bills;
His oaks bore pewter acorns that unscrewed.

Increase perfection! So, he shaped a wife,
  Pleated the fabric of her chartered thigh,
Begat sons by excisions of a knife
  In camphorwood. He warned them not to die.

The moment flowed. So did his cellophane
  Brook over rollers. All obdurate day
  His player-piano tunkled him its lay,
Though on its ivory dentures a profane

Tarnish kept ripening, and where high tide
  Slid on ballbearings ceaselessly to shore,
Red rust. All night, the world that lolled outside
  Kept thrusting newborn rats under his door.

Cross Ties

Out walking ties left over from a track
Where nothing travels now but rust and grass,
I could take stock in something that would pass
Bearing down Hell-bent from behind my back:
A thing to sidestep or go down before,
Far-off, indifferent as that curfew's wail
The evening wind flings like a sack of mail
Or close up as the moon whose headbeam stirs
A flock of cloud to make tracks. Down to strafe
Bristle-backed grass a hawk falls—there's a screech
Like steel wrenched taut till severed. Out of reach
Or else beneath desiring, I go safe,
Walk on, tensed for a leap, unreconciled
To a dark void all kindness.
                                        When I spill
The salt I throw the Devil some and, still,
I let them sprinkle water on my child.

For a Maiden Lady

A tremor in her wrist
Forbade us to exist.
Fevers arose to burn
Her few twigs. All concern
Run past, her look congealed
Like a spare boudoir sealed
Against the gilt snuff box,
Lavengro, the lace clocks
She had crocheted when able,
The postcard on the table,
Chrysanthemums still damp,
The stopped moth by the lamp,
All we who had played kind,
So much dust thrust from mind.

Transparency

Love was the woman I loved,
A grave, inhuman woman.
At night in our room alone,
I, self-sufficient Adam,
Laid hand on my cold bone.

She could unhook her face
And, smiling, lay it down,
Pick up a living face
That wobbled in her hand
And smooth it into place.

She'd turn on me dim lips
Held to my lips by will,
Yet, as she thinned to sleep,
Even through gorged eyes
I could see through her skull.

Giving In to You

Laird of a makeshift castle,
Drawbridge trussed up tight,
I sat supplanting light,
Hard striving to be facile.

I wrote a book. It dried.
I stood it on my shelf
And feasted, pride
A mouth swallowing the body from around itself.

Now I give in to you
As the house of the county poor's
Gauze curtains do
To the luxurious wind
That, knowing how to be kind,
Overflows all outdoors.

Among Stool Pigeons

Falling between two stools, his forehead cracked
　Hard on the finger-painters' bench. The sums
Like hay caught in a hurricane came unstacked.
　From head to foot he felt himself all thumbs.

Oddly enough, the lesson plan went on.
　Brim-full of gin, he watched the ceiling: wheels
Skipped from their axle. Sprawled in a cold stun,
　Expecting Miss Runcible's smart peck of heels,

Foresaw the Board meet, beetle-browed: *"The rap
　Is moral turp, twerp—what you got to say?"*
"Fongoo."
　　　"Guards! Seize him!"
　　　　　"Catch me!"
　　　　　　　End your yawp
　And come away,

You hoot-owl treading snow,
　Quit. When the weight of that soaked hulk you are
Breaks through the crust, you might as well let go.
　This stuff's for wrens to tiptoe on. The car

Has one more payment due—rouse! Christ, I'm crocked,
　Old head's all puddles . . . Glenda had to go . . .
Here comes that star-splashed dark . . . Was I half-cocked
　To give the pigeons *Opium* by Cocteau?

　　　　*　*　*

Upon his mouth the children, twittering, wove
　A second mouth before they stole away
To tell on him and kindly pressed it there:
　Corners turned down, light blue, of modeling clay.

Loose Woman

Someone who well knew how she'd toss her chin
   Passing the firehouse oglers, at their taunt,
   Let it be flung up higher than she'd want,
Just held fast by a little hinge of skin.
Two boys come from the river kicked a thatch
   Of underbrush and stopped. One wrecked a pair
   Of sneakers blundering into her hair
And that day made a different sort of catch.

Her next-best talent—setting tongues to buzz—
   Lasts longer than her best. It still occurs
   To wonder had she been our fault or hers
And had she loved him. Who the bastard was,
Though long they asked and notebooked round about
   And turned up not a few who would have known
   That white inch where her neck met shoulderbone,
Was one thing more we never did find out.

Absentminded Bartender

He'd meant to scare her, just, not hurt,
Who would have thought so light a tap . . . ?
Hey, you asleep?
           He gave a start,
Cut off head dribbling from the tap.

Cities and hotels
Since then had made one corridor
Of bulbs, extinguishers. Somewhere else
Was where he hung out more and more,
And drinking, though it made days worse,
Blurred how it had been, looking back,
And made time harder to reverse
Unless he had an egg to crack
And burst the yolk of.
                In his room,
Sunlight locked out, there sought for ease
In fresh positions legs and arms
Severed, alive, in bed with his.

Two Apparitions

1

Half in dreams, half with me, she lay: some foal
    Hardly born. As I crossed her spine
With a hand, out to join it and bind her stole
    Another man's hand, not mine,

A scaled hand, a lizard's, blotched over with bile,
    Every knuckle a knot on a stick,
And in her cheek, dug there, a crone's wan smile.
    I shuddered. Wild-eyed she woke,

Then in the next moment, the moon's white rise
    Cast the two of us smooth once more
And we fell to each other with timid cries,
    Backs turned on what lay in store.

2

Where no man laid eyes,
Down our bedroom wall
Slid the head of the moon
Like a genital
Hardly able to rise,
Too cold to assuage
Having had to look on
In diseased old age.

Poets

These people are . . . quenched. I mean the natives.
D. H. Lawrence, letter of 14 August 1923
from Dover, New Jersey.

Le vierge, le vivace, et le bel aujourd'hui . . .

What were they like as schoolboys? Long on themes
And short of wind, perpetually outclassed,
Breaking their glasses, always chosen last
    When everyone was sorted out in teams,

Moody, a little dull, the kind that squirmed
At hurt cats, shrank from touching cracked-up birds,
With all but plain girls at a loss for words,
    Having to ask to have their fishhooks wormed,

Snuffers of candles every priest thought nice,
Quenchers of their own wicks, their eyes turned down
And smoldering. In Dover, my home town,
    No winter passed but we had swans in ice,

Birds of their quill: so beautiful, so dumb,
They'd let a window glaze about their feet,
Not seeing through their dreams till time to eat.
    A fireman with a blowtorch had to come

Thaw the dopes loose. Sun-silvered, plumes aflap,
Weren't they grand, though? Not that you'd notice it,
Crawling along a ladder, getting bit,
    Numb to the bone, enduring all their crap.

The Korean Emergency

Under Mount Etna's shadow, the Exec
In apoplexy on the quarterdeck
Razzing the OD,
                           Boy, for Chrissake clear
These guineas out of here,
                                    our destroyer swung,
A broody sow hard set on by her shoats,
Bumboats,
The oiled tide
Swelling a moment only to subside,
Hesitant as breath from an injured lung.

All shat shaved shoeshined showered-off, each bore
His wait for boatspace, out for his own turn
To hit the beach with fifty bucks to burn.
Spilling from floating nests their fathers poled,
Sharp-beaked bambinos in wrapped-rag shoes tore
Through GI cans for our potato peels,
Shivering. Although it didn't seem too cold.

We'd only to desire and they'd desire.
We rolled our stones, they gathered in our moss.
How not to admire
That one-eyed painter never at a loss
Given the dimmest wallet-snapshot? Lo,
Back came the spitting image of your girl
Staring in oils, ringed with a holy glow,
Eerie, some stranded pearl
Bloated a yard across.
A round red token like a meat-ration point
You gave the broad and, afterward, made whole,
Blessed with a pro kit from the Shore Patrol,
Tackled the guided tour of Syracuse,
Its Roman theater some crab's

Picked gutted shell. Let loose,
The lira leaking out of your dress blues,
You'd wander, up for grabs,
Through droves of boys who'd feel you out and pluck,
Or, if it were your will
Down on the beach or under some dark arch,
Nurse or give suck.

Who'd hate a thirst that held him in its sway
When the deep wine dish of the Mediterranean lay
Within his hands? Once more
We steamed back home. To meet us on the dock
Sat Gene's Dry Cleans.
                    Emergency, not war.

West Somerville, Mass.

1 DAY 7

Sundays we wake to tumbrils: iron wheels
Crack pebbles as they mount through Somerville's
Evasive sunshine. Round our blinded room,
From wall to wall reverberations drum:
Our newsboy with his railway baggage cart
Toils Medford Hill, up past the bleeding heart
Of the doll stuck in Apicelli's lawn,
Bearing the fat white body of the *Globe*
That comes in sections like a sacred robe,
Swearing as though he had it in for dawn.

The boy's breath coarsens, torn forth from his ribs.
They're sitting up now, crowing in their cribs,
Throwing things. I quit my dozing wife,
Fumble tied shoestrings—O Lord, for a knife!—
Raise broken blinds, let daylight trickle through.
What was it, once, I used to have to do?
This day means beef not ground, and unmade dollar,
This day means Mutt and Jeff will come in color,
Time to feed tame ducks stale crusts, freed from pressure
As shaving cream sprung from its can. Let's raze.
Deep in the mirror I confront two eyes
Like the last windowpanes you'd see in blocks
Doomed to renewal, so far spared boys' rocks.

2 THE ASCENT

The rock rolled back, the stained race hatched out new,
They pass my window, the communicants,

Each with two neat knife-edges in his pants.
In bathrobe still, out of it as a Jew,

Wonder Bread toast, cold coffee at my teeth,
I mark time on a half-baked villanelle
That will not rise. Lord knows, up Medford Hill
I'd go, but stop short before that wraith

My body risen, back, the old hale fellow,
All the same hangnails, chilblains, the whole bit,
Arms out for soul to re-embrace with it.
He'd be hard tack to swallow,

And, feet fast rotting, how to toe the line
On Mary's hoist to Heaven? Call it myth,
But that's pale stuff to slake a body with,
Water after Pope John's wine.

My faith copped out. Who was it pulled that heist?
Wasn't it me, too stuck-up and aloof
To spill my sins? If knocked on for a roof,
I wouldn't have a chair to offer Christ,

But He'd no more halt at my door than they,
Unless to frown in on my snotty kids
Aping their bonnets, sporting potty lids.
One dark duenna screws up lips to slay

Me with a word. Peace, Momma!—I'd go back
To forehead ashes, giving up for Lent,
But I gave up every blessed sacrament.
Can the strait gate still stand open a crack?

Who'd grudge joy to an angel, if it can?
Last night in the bathtub, groping for the soap,

I tried a sloppy act of love, felt hope
Drum at my heart with vague feet. Pregnant man,

What's eating you? Good Friday, on to plunge
His lance, a soldier stepped in, drove up hard,
Laughed and drew back. The captain of the guard
Offered a vinegar-soaked sponge.

Again, eventual as spring, some goodman begs
The Body, decks it out in his own tomb,
Limbs in clean linen, wounds touched with sweet balm.
It took place while I shopped for Easter eggs.

O lukewarm spew, you, stir yourself and boil
Or be not chosen. Strike with your whole weight
At hook, line, sinker—be fished, or cut bait—
Give, or get off the pot—

My hope steps up. He bites the loosening ear
Of his milk-chocolate rabbit. Limb from limb
The victim's rendered. Let us eat of him
Some other year.

Each dawn the children rout me out. What profit
To shrink back like a dumb bulb? At a loss,
I stretch out arms, fix feet as on a cross
Till something says, *Come off it.*

3   GOLGOTHA
    (1968)

Grey fur collars on a steel limb,
The welders, keeping hands warm
Inside their sheet-plastic cocoon,
Weave the new dorm
Late into night, deadlined
For April. According to plan,

The chewed hill's to be redefined
And seedlings, to a man,
Stood up in ranks to face blight,
Green lawn unrolled,
Brick walls, adolescently bright,
Sprayed to look old.

In my locked childproof basement work room,
Furnace vapors
Chase their own tails. Roof-high, loom
Ungraded papers.
An iron door in a brick wall
A kick could splinter
Dikes back the ashes of all
Our hearths of winter.
I half-hear the thrash of bed sheets,
A mouse scratch, taking chances.
Down the spine of my dogeared John Keats
Mildew advances.

Cramped handwriting, don't know his name:
How Youth Is Shafted
By Society—now I've pegged him,
They got him. Drafted.
(Through vines in a gnarled neutral zone,
A locust nation,
Flamethrowers grazing, moves on
About its task, defoliation.)
Interesting idea, says my pen
To a John Bircher—liar, liar!—
Shots rattle. No, the stuffed lion's
Brass eyeballs in the dryer.

I take out trash, not to read more—
Torn gift wraps, Christmas-tree rain—
Lift can-cover on a white horde
Writhing. Lean rain
Blown to bits by the murderous wind

Has it in for you, finger and face,
Drives through every hole to your brain,
Taking over the place
As though it had been here before,
Had come back in its own hour,
Snow gaining ground in the dark yard,
The mad in absolute power.

Intermission

LIGHT VERSE

Lewis Carroll

Click! down the black whiterabbithole
Of his light-tight box he swooped
Liddell girls (women in capsule form,
My dear the better to eat you).

On tiptoe past intimidated primroses,
His head ateeter on its collar wall,
The Reverend Mr Dodgson longdivided
God's cipher (1 goes 3 × into 3)

And shrinking as his Alice grew, rejected
The little flask of love that said *Drink Me.*

Rondel

Violation on a theme by Charles d'Orléans

The world is taking off her clothes
  Of snowdrift, rain, and strait-laced freeze
  And turns, to show forth by degrees
The bosom of a Rose La Rose.

There's not a bud nor bird, Lord knows,
  Can stay still in boughs' balconies.
The world is taking off her clothes
  Of snowdrift, rain, and strait-laced freeze.

Brooklet grown great from melting snows
  Wears a g-string of ice to tease
  And, sequined, river's last chemise
Undone in a shudder goes.
The world is taking off her clothes.

Categories

Nothing stays put: the copra-eating apes
Drop from their trees to sup on centipedes;
Species collide like fast tailgating cars;
Milksops cut teeth; no sooner is the course
In Post-Arnoldian Prose Style xeroxed up
Than styles expire, essential stylists change
Sexes or nations. On the strand
Mollusks the ocean punches drunk relax
Their clasps, turn butterflies.

The century bunches and, like hurrying sand,
Collapses through the mind's pained hourglass.
Was it Rimbaud, that trader of tusks, who said
You don't begin to understand
Till through the tip of your tongue you hear bright red?
Recall that master in Kyoto who began
"To seize on what had been left out before"
When one of the novice monks, a scrubber of pots,
Proved with a simple wrist-flick that you can,
If you have hatched from names, or lack clean plates,
Serve cake on a shut fan.

Carrying On Without Him

As if the blows of ten-ton trucks
   Were what one took in stride,
Not even staggered in their tracks,
   His shoes with strings still tied

Stepped giant through a greenhouse pane
   As if they'd choose therein
Commemorations for the man
   Whose bearers they had been.

The florist goggled. Reined up short,
   The left shoe took its stand,
The right arced up: a pot of dirt
   Imploded in his hand.

Pedestrians two such as these,
   How could one grow to love?—
Pure shoes below the displaced knees,
   Dismounted air above.

Now who would think two leather graves,
   The clods we rise to don,
Could shrug us, no more be our slaves,
   And footloose carry on?

Absorbed, an empire leaps too late
   And while the brake still squeals
Some flunky trampled underfoot
   Starts kicking up his heels.

The Aged Wino's Counsel
to a Young Man on the Brink of Marriage

A two-quart virgin in my lap,
With hands that shook I peeled her cap
And filched a kiss. It warmed me so,
I raised my right hand, swore *I do*—
We merged our fleshes, I and she,
In mutual indignity.

Now, when I hear of wives that freeze,
Bitter of lip, with icebound knees,
Who play high-card for social bets
And lose, and feed you carp croquettes,
Who nap all day and yak all night
What Ruth told Min—now which was right?—
Who count with glee your falling hairs
But brood a week on one of theirs,
Who'll see your parkerhouse poke out
Before they'll take a stitch, who pout
At change of moon, as I hear tell,
I say: son, wed you half so well.

The Phantom of Woodland Homes

Steamshovel forceps creak,
Budge the entrenched stump—
Its gums smoothed, now the hill smiles
With artificial timber.

But even now some nights
When white TVs in phases gleam
From every sunken livingroom,
The final child bestowed to bed,
There comes a ghost with beaver teeth,
Gobbets of fungus-moss for hair
And hootowl holes instead of eyes,
Who drifts the snippered breezeways, steals
Through parked cars strewing porcupines
In glove compartment and back seat—

At dawn his hawk-clawed prints surround
Petunias stifled in their plots,
The tricycle found tied in knots.

The Medium Is the Message

Plugged in, stone deaf, sleepwalking into trains,
Teenagers die, transistors stuck to their brains,
Steps locked to rock, each mind a listening post,
At break of station giving up the ghost.

The rude beast slouches. Shall each babe at birth
Be operated on and belted forth
With aerial implanted, his own screen,
And, turned on, watch late late shows in his bean?
Then, words in lines may be as obsolete
As hand-carved airships driven by steam heat.

Fresh beats the age insists on—not the heart's,
But those of rush-hour traffic's fits and starts.
Would I then drop out of my times? You bet!—
Could I but pack along my hi-fi set,
Electric light, a crate of books, canned beer
To help keep medieval ardor clear.
Then, hunched at my quill I'd blow cold thumbs perhaps
Lest one word of Yeats lapse.

Pottery Class

On Wednesday nights, the children rinsed and stacked,
The wives, their husbands closeted with *Time*,
From Lexington and Concord motor in
To travail in this elemental slime.

Thwack! and a hunk of muck hung by the heels
Has its back slapped, its breathing made to come.
Great casseroles take shape on groaning wheels.
A vase commences, vast as Christendom.

Women, what's eating you? What is it drives
Your hands to forage, take up earth to knit?
Dull flickswitch chores? The drag of being wives?
The deep grave that a birth leaves after it?

Lay waste your manicures now though you may,
Yours is that furious core man stands outside,
Gazing, stone-helpless while you firm his clay
And bask him in your kilns until he's dried.

Reunion

Impassive, to a tuba chord,
  Their faces blurred like photostats,
Enter the class of '34
  In wheelchairs, coned with paper hats.

Discreet, between the first Scotch punch
  And the last tot of buttered rum,
President Till works over each
  Fomenting his new stadium.

Fire in one eye, the class tycoon,
  Four hog-hairs bristling from his chin,
Into his neighbor's Sonotone
  Confides his plan to corner tin.

His waitress with a piercing squeal
  Wrests loose a buttock from his grip.
Dropping the napkins a good deal,
  She titters, puddling ox-tail soup.

Now all, cranked high, shrill voices raise
  To quaver strains of purple hills
'Neath Alma Mater's book of days.
  Some dim sub-dean picks up the bills—

One last car door slam breaks a whine
  Solicitous of someone's health,
And softly through the mezzanine
  The night revives with punctual stealth.

Drivers of Diaper Service Trucks Are Sad

Drivers of diaper service trucks are sad:
They dredge their pails for wet ones lying loose
As if both they and women had been had.

If stock-cars were their steeds, would they be glad,
Not jerk a sack shut like a hangman's noose?
Drivers of diaper service trucks are sad.

You'd think childbearing but a passing fad
From which they wring a temporary juice
As if both they and women had been had,

And had, and had. How can our earth be glad
To bear the brunt of one more brat's abuse?
Drivers of diaper service trucks are sad.

That day I phoned in answer to their ad,
How could I know? Must men help reproduce
As if both they and women had been had?

Truck engines snarl. And leave you clutching, dad,
Bundles of spanking white ones. What's the use?
Drivers of diaper service trucks are sad
As if both they and women had been had.

Robert Frost Discovers Another Road Not Taken

Two roads diverged in a wood
As though in argument.
I had to keep going on one
To get to the end of a scent
That a nostril had begun,
But I picked out the no good.

What did it lead me to?
The old moose chewing her teat.
Still I'm bound to put up with Fate
Despite that aftermath.
I'd hold out for some kind of path
Under a body's feet.

Two Views of Rhyme and Meter

1

What's meter
but the thud
    thud
    thud of a bent wire
carpetbeater

fogging the air
with boredom
in dull time

and the dust,
rhyme?

2

Meter
Is the thrust rest thrust of loins and peter
And rhyme,
To come at the same time.

In a Dry Season

Willing to rise yet weighed down with thought,
I am that early would-be aeronaut
Who strives to mount the clouds, but only walks,
Flapping upholstered arms, emitting squawks.

And why do I, who yearn to straddle stars,
Toy with drained steins in unswept singles' bars?
Descend, O Muse. Bestow, ungracious slattern.
Quit circling Boston in a holding pattern.

Gold Bought Here

Clutching old gauds and baubles up for sale,
 With fellow sellers-out I stand in queue.
Time having washed aside nostalgia's shale,
 I grope for nuggets in its residue.

Who's next? A bride of long ago twists loose
 Her wedding band, relinquishing a weight
That, all the while love's worth had done its nose-
 Dive, had to glitter and appreciate.

Thick-skinned, our buyers spurn mere plate. No deal
 For Aunt Beth's tooth, the school ring whose vined brass
Looks overgrown with weeds—just how I feel—
 Missing both stones. Fit emblem for its class.

Now farewell, bright medallion—SECOND OUTSTAND-
 ING STUDENT 1950 DEP'T OF ED.—
Bestowed me from an old archbishop's hand
 I had to kiss. Snippered, its heart proves lead.

Then hollowed, like some walker of the street
 Lightened of his one talent, paid by check,
I step outside. Cold neon-lighted sleet
 Nibbles with costly fillings at my neck.

III

1969–1971

Traveler's Warnings

MAIN ROAD WEST

The Late Late Show, rebounding from the hill
That screens the rundown town, gives up its ghost:
A screen star ancient as this Oak Motel
Undergoes facelifts—loses voice—is lost.
The channel slithers from the set's blunt hook.
No magazines. No book but the Good Book.

Half-parted drapes, snapped lock, and a long drink
In a glass meant for water. Almost gone,
Trees that grow leaves, as though you'd crossed a brink.
The wind's turned off. The sign USED CARS stays on
That keeps hard stars from piercing through to town,
As though stars will be foresworn, or stared down.

EDGAR'S STORY

What we'd been missing out on all those years
Of stoking up the coffeepot at dawn,
Those Sundays, sitting working on some beers,
Watching the sprinkler going on the lawn
Was what we wanted. Gassed the old tin can
And lit out up the turnpike, Nell and I,
Soon as I got my fourteen-karat pen
And pencil set, and wrote, and it went dry.

Woods were the good part: straight up, all their limbs
Creaking with leaves. But then we'd have to go
Gawk at some china plates and hand-carved looms.
Freight cars sat idling, sad towns in their tow
And snake farms where you stood and looked at snakes.
Now all those plastic squirrels that say, *I'm nuts*

For the Dakota Bad Lands on their butts,
That nobody laughs at, long, give me cold shakes.

Somehow out there with not much else around
In the motel at night, it starts to hurt,
Thinking, and your head beginning to pound
In time to the drip-drying of your shirt,
Of redwood forests melted down for pulp.
It ties a knot in my bowels
Every time I cost a branch to take a crap
And dry my hands off on some paper towels.

At Mount Rushmore I looked up into one
Of those faces born joined to the same neck bone.
I said, *Abe, Abe, how does it feel to be up there?*—
And that rock he has for a pupil budged, I swear,
And he looked me in the eye and he said, *Alone.*

NATIONAL SHRINE

Sanctioned by eagles, this house. Here they'd met,
Undone their swordbelts, smoked awhile and posed
Gazes that could not triumph or forget,
And held their jowls set till a shutter closed.

Kentucky rifle now, and Parrot gun
Cohabit under glass. Connecticut
And Alabama, waxed sleek in the sun,
Reflect like sisters in the parking lot.

Lee's troops led home to gutted field and farm
Mules barely stumbling. Borne off in each car,
The wounded sun and instant Kodachrome
Render our truces brighter than they are.

PEACE AND PLENTY

Bound to the road by chains
Of motels, hills of pines
Under the moon lie stunned.
An Adirondack stirs
Winds, groping for her firs.
Engines are gunned

And, not knowing which path to choose
Through the chemical plant, the river
Choked with refuse
Upturns a blithering stare
To the exhausted air.
Crows hover.

Let the new fallen snow
Before she change her mind
Lay bare her body to the Presto-Blo,
The drooped rose her
Quietus find
Head down inside the in-sink waste-disposer.

ANT TRAP

Innocuous as a clock, giving off whiffs
Of roast beef rare and tubs brim-full of gin
Free to the rank and file of working stiffs,
This Siren in a tin can lures them in.
A skull-and-crossbones on her lid warns men
Not to crack up against her reefs,
But how could that turn back an ant, his skin
Already bone, to whom death's head is life's?

Out through her punctured doors, down winding roads,
Each totes his doom home and his kinsmen's doom

In trust. Recall those fourteen-year-old broads
Who'd stand across the street from Napoleon's Tomb
Beckoning not with fingers but perfume
The worn GI in quest of other wars
And kinder arms than guns to come home from,
Remember how they'd stretch forth open pores.

Not that the gift he fetched home was the clap—
Although he might have—no, nor just the can
Of Spanish fly our good Rotarian
Smuggled back home to storm the girlfriend's lap,
No dirtybook, no head cut from a Jap
Scrubbed to a whitened skull in some latrine,
Nothing to shove a pin through on a map,
But wider than all France's *belle poitrine*.

And now, kempt creature treading in straight files,
Social, in press, his jawbone razored sleek,
Hopping the shuttle daily, vaulting miles
To and from Montauk, hearing the same rails click,
Delivered nightly back to his Blest Isles,
Do his nerves go slack,
Does he sip with glazed eyeballs and cast smile
His scotch-and-water in a state of shock,

Or find, perhaps, death ill disposed to come
And slow death a far cry from what he needs?
All his beliefs dead leaves for turning from,
His sons mock. Minds expanded on mad creeds
Nurtured by moon in Katmandu, they bloom
Like vines that crack their temple steps, burn weed,
Smoke and explode the sunken livingroom
And sooner than they'd hear him, die from speed.

Then too, the failure's failure: twitching, scared,
Starving for more than fingers ever plucked.
In one fixed bar you'll find him stoutly chaired,
Gulping the day's war rumor, pissing fact,

His days one downhill slide from having warred
On others than himself. Vague hands extract
Invisible bayonets. He'll show the world—
Clean out the bastards! (he and beer reflect).

So, by their weakening lights you guess how all
That army shuttling through it in a train
With nothing but its sweetness on one brain
Must feel when, home, their heartbeats falter and stall—
When, clutching sides, they double up in pain
And, footholds loosening, they begin to fall,
Cast forth faint feelers, grope, catch fast again:
Stiffening columns in behind a wall.

BEST SELLER

The copy we'd sent off for, on its rounds
Growing dog-eared, the pack of us in there
Saw ourselves whipped and, smarting from our wounds,
Took to our legs and bayed. In Courthouse Square
Faster and faster till the dustclouds spun
Our spastic schoolbus driver gunned his bus
On finding out that he had put him in
And made him out the one whole man of us.

So mad we hitched a scarecrow to a limb,
Set it on fire and tore its britches down,
We could light on no names too low for him—
That is, until the guided tours hit town,
Bought two-bit tickets to the chickencoop
Old Wylie'd rigged to pass off for the scene
Of the big gang-bang, ate our tall tales up
And guzzled us bone-dry of gasoline.

Well. This was different. So we nailed up boards
To show where he'd been born and had lived last,
Rooted a stunty peach tree in the yard

Where Elfa's baby fires the shotgun blast
That unmans its own father, passed the hat
And set a granite skullcap on the head
Of Scholar Alpaugh's statue—did all that
To put things more in line with how he'd said.

We might have known. The nameplate of the town
High on the depot wall has flaked so dim
You have to squint at it. We'd take it down
And paint it fresh, but, on account of him,
We're written up in guidebooks now, and, stuck,
We ghost about the daylight feeling thin,
Like stolen bones that ought to be put back.
Only one train, now, bothers down our track.

Hot nights when sleep holds off, in the one bar,
Called Elfa's Nest, chairs propped up to the wall,
Watching the ash of Horace Coe's cigar
Hang on like one last rubberneck's eyeball,
We don't talk much. The whole town's on a shelf,
Thick under webs no hand's about to muss.
Just the wind making echoes to itself,
The wind, the parched wind goes on fingering us.

WHAT SHE TOLD THE SHERIFF

Hot nights out in the cornshocks,
    Snakelike they'd go
Bashing about in pickup trucks,
    Headlights on low,
Staking out soft beds in Hell,
    Giggling. Till morning,
Safe on my windowsill,
    I'd do the darning,
Three-way lamp all the way up,
    Hymns turned on louder,
Knees tight locked, china cup
    Of headache powder

Running over. I'd kiss Christ
  (My own right arm)
Or read till, my eyes crossed,
  Red words would squirm.
I'd pray: Change places, Lord,
  Stroke by stroke the corn
Watches You nailed back on Your board
  Sure as You're born.
Lend me the power to damn
  Those lipsticked, caving
Doors to man's battering-ram.
  What one's worth saving?—
No sign. Only the moon's gleam,
  Monotonous tick talk
From the wall clock, shine of ice cream
  Bowls from the dish rack,
Four years locked in a frame
  Instead of marriage:
The sheepskin bearing my name
  Like some miscarriage.
Paul said, *Our days in earth
  Are as a shadow* . . .
Father no doubt slept with
  His plump grass-widow
While Mother courted sleep,
  As ever ailing,
Spending life's ocean trip
  Hugged to the railing.
Next noon, out choosing ears
  For the lunch pot,
I'd come on sin's arrears
  Still body-hot:
There in the scrambled dirt
  The telltale pressings
Of buttocks, a torn-off shirt,
  Love's smelly passings.
Father, how could Your Hand
  Deign to forgive?

Smite them! Don't understand,
  Don't just let live!
I'd weep, the sun's broadsword
  Carving my bonnet,
For this blood-handed world
  And all here on it.
Then one noon, my Maker's ways
  Laid themselves bare.
Scabs fell down from my eyes,
  All stood forth clear:
Worms, worms in leaf and ear,
  Kernel and tassel,
Gnawing the Wurlitzer
  In Burger Castle!
Hell peered through surgeon's slits,
  Burst out of faucets—
Babies chopped off at the root,
  Crushed flat in corsets!
My heart caught fire in me,
  Fire hard to cover—
How endlessly time marks time
  When God's your lover—
And it was all I could do
  Till my right hour
To hold a lid over my glow,
  Sifting cake flour.
Midnight. Led by my sword,
  Ripe for reborning,
I strode in where Dad snored,
  Mother lay turning:
Two old and swollen sheep
  Stretched out for slaughter,
Teeth set adrift to keep
  In mineral water,
They were like chopping wood.
  Drunk, uncomplaining,
And wondering Dad stood
  A long while draining.

Mother half raised her, coughed,
   Said—for once painless—
Girl, wipe that cleaver off,
   That one's not stainless.
Next, blazing kerosene
   Smote the brown oily
Head-shaped time-honored stain
   From Dad's chair doily.
Along the henhouse path,
   Dry faggots crackled.
At each step I shook earth with
   The bantam cackled.
Saint Michael goaded me,
   Grass fire his halo,
Render unto Your Father on high
   Your father's silo!
Wrath roared in my right hand,
   How soon it catched
Where, like deceivers' tents,
   Hay sat pitched.
Creatures of hoof and horn,
   Sheol's lumps of tallow,
Struck at the walls of their barn
   That soon grew hollow.
Far as earth led the eye,
   Smoke bloomed, burnt stubble
Crawled legless. It was I
   Cast down the Devil.
Why do you handcuff me?
   Let go! By morning
All Iowa could be
   One high bush, burning.

THE SELF-EXPOSED

On the Bangor-bound platform, the crowd became one
Shaping lips to me: *Now, sweet, now!*—

On the handle of my zipper, my hand dragged down,
Out it budded, my golden bough

In that plate-glass proscenium my Pullman room.
An old biddy guffawed, a valise
Being handed up to a conductor's hand
Blossomed underwear, a man yelled *Police!*—

Then we lurched, I was gone. What gets into me?
I'm not one to be peter-proud,
But my bird-out-of-hand longs to take its stand
On the farther side from what's allowed.

People with their foreheads like income tax forms
Raise the puke in me! How I yearn
To scribble with my dibble on their neat-ruled norms.
They'll nail me yet. I never learn.

Oh, I've been to psychiatrist and priest,
I've read an uplifting book,
But it's cold, and I hunger to walk forth dressed
In the quilt of the world's warm look.

DRIVING CROSS-COUNTRY

Jack Giantkiller took and struck
    His harp and stalks sat up, all ears—
With wavelengths corn in Keokuk
    Comes on so hard it interferes.

Glass vacant, in the Stoplight Lounge,
    Expecting to be stood a meal,
Ella Ashhauler has to scrounge,
    Her slipper tilted, for some heel.

Where is the prince of yesteryear
    Beneath whose lip princesses roused?

Bourbon will add a gleam of cheer.
The place has lately been deloused.

Prints of a bowling-ball-eyed child
Brood over ornamental pewter.
A wand's been waved, the whole house styled
To offend no one, by computer:

A room the same as last night's room,
Exact same bath mat underfoot.
In thrall to some unlucky charm,
We hurtle, but, it seems, stay put.

When, headlight-blind, we let fall head
On pillows hard by right-hand lanes
In airconditioned gingerbread,
It keeps on driving through our veins,

Some hag's black broth. At dawn we stare,
Locked into lane by rule of lime.
We had a home. It was somewhere.
We were there once upon a time.

READING TRIP

Everybody's in po biz.
    Louis Simpson

Just past a grove where roots in overthrow
    Work air for nothing and boughs lie, still clung
With oranges stopped short, the towers show,
    Slim exhalations from a plastic lung,
        Shimmering distinctly: knowledge reared with pride.
        Whose Hell is here? Nutt's letter for my guide,

I ask the straight way to the English Dep't
    Of girls too beautiful ever to be of use,
Wondering by what husbandry they're kept

Golden and huge, aburst with squeezing juice.
The secretary, withered on her bough,
Unclicks a gate latch: *"Mister Nutt's yours now."*

A handshake, hearty, fingers a little stiff
(From years of etching grades on freshmanese?),
A pool-cue-following eye, though. Kind as if
I'd been John Clare, or one of the Trustees.
Miss Cone will Beatrice me to the hall.
God bless Nutt, there'll be liquor after all.

With buzzer Nutt invokes his teaching bard
Whose class has just let out: who gropes at length
For the right gambit, picking his key word.
He's read me, I've read him. Testing his strength,
Each circles each, protecting his behind,
Not knowing, sniffing after his own kind.

I'm in his hands for—what? A temperance lunch
With all our eyebeams stuck fast to our plates?
With namecards, with the Tuesday-Thursday bunch
Mulling the phases of the moon of Yeats?
Jerusalem set free! he knows a bar
For hot corned beef! *"Come on, I've got a car."*

And there in the click and hush of shuffleboard,
Bridging our distances with pitcher-beer,
Something not far from sour truth being poured,
Each makes out what the other has to bear.
Close as a brace of long-lost concubines,
We drink up, and misquote each other's lines.

After I'm let to stop off at the john,
It's time to do my poet act, the house
A thin fourth filled and looking put upon,
Except for one attentive-as-a-mouse
Pale braided lass with twitching button nose.
Nutt rallies all to man the front-line rows.

I offer Hardy's "Ruined Maid," on watch
  For hints of acquiescence. About half
Coolly endure, let out their yawns a notch;
    Some look about—are they supposed to laugh?
      But here and there, a grin, unprepossessed,
      Shimmers, a lump of ore that's passed its test.

And after, the popcorn-burst of handclaps spent,
  Will some hang on? Why, sure as Hell, released,
A few struggle forward, bold or hesitant,
    The better to read the fine print on the beast.
      Pale Mouse steals up on tiptoe and I'm slipped
      A morsel of her own mauve manuscript.

"How do you get ideas to write about?"—
  I fumble for the old stuffed-owl replies:
*"Oh I don't know, I guess I just start out
    With a few words that match." "What market buys
      Ballads on water sports?"*—my shoulders sag.
      "Don't you find rhyming everything a drag?"

A drag, man? Worse than that! Between the eyes,
  I take the blade of his outrageous stare.
Whoever crosses him, the varlet dies,
    Trapped Guest to his unancient Mariner:
      *"Get with it, baby, what you want to be
      So artsy-craftsy for? Screw prosody,*

*"Turn it on, man, it's like for now, today,
  Disposable stuff, word-Kleenex. Why take pains
Trimming it neat? Nobody gonna play
    That game no more."* A man worth crossing brains
      And tanking up with, wrestling with all night—
      But not tonight, man. Let me off tonight.

The bard reprieves me. Soon there's clinking ice
  And bourbon in suburbia, a haze
Of settled evening. Out of artifice,

Sated with me and all my works and days,
I guess what drove one Welsh bard wild to squeeze
Buttock and bottle. Miss Cone cuts blue cheese.

And here, in this kindly orchard of the blest,
Whose pretext for a stiff drink I have been,
This tenured, literate Oktoberfest
That even paid to let me make its scene,
Earth, it appears, will be bare earth indeed
When they're chopped down, the last ones left who'll read.

Recloistered in the dry cell of my car,
Ego discharging back to natural size,
I grope for balance, break off and discard
Like petals of an artichoke, the lies
I stick out with all over, fumbling for
A means to shrivel back to some sort of core,

Edge out into the dusk to claim my slot
In the home-droning traffic, less and less
The bard on fire, more one now with the blot
That hoods the stars above Los Angeles,
Hard gunning, on the make for far-off nights,
Like any other pair of downcast brights.

O'Riley's Late-Bloomed Little Son

O'Riley's late-bloomed little son,
Shown off for seven weeks,
Frostbitten, shrank back in again.
They'd picked him up to find out if
His croup would stop, them holding him,
But in their arms he just went stiff.

They say she's past her change of life.
You'll see them Saturdays
In the back yard, her breaking ground
For a white birch, him on a mound
No higher than that where their hope lies,
Reaching, cold beer in other hand,
For Lucille and Camille's pop flies.

Daughter in the House

This sleeping face, not even mine nor yours,
A hard thing to have charge of, not to own,
Settled on us through time, as ocean floors
Bestow them in long snowfalls made of bone:
A face half foreign, half of some we know,
Borne down upon her, as a gem occurs
Out of the first leaves ever tree let go,
From tons that crushed dead faces into hers.

Smooth as the skin laid on a pail of cream,
Her sleep hides ferment. Would we work her wrong
To lift it off and peer in on her dream?
Hasn't she been down in herself too long?
But no. Two pools abused by thunderbursts,
We regain balance in her quiet spells.
She is our drink. It was for her our thirsts
Singled out each other's wells.

The Shorter View

Her eyes outstretched from seeing how in space
Stars in old age will stagger, drop, and burst,
Throwing out far their darknesses and dust,
My wife lets her book fall with stricken face.
She'd thought tomorrow set and rooted here,
And people. That some morning will occur
Without a sunrise hadn't dawned on her.
Kathleen some great pink shell held to her ear,
And, wistful, staring through me to an earth
Littered with ashes, too dried-up to bear—
Though I say, *What the Hell, we won't be there*—
She doesn't see much point in giving birth
And, in our dark bed where her burden grew,
When I'd make love and recklessly let live,
Her arms drawn shut, for this night will not give
One inch of ground for any shorter view.

Ode

Old tumbril rolling with me till I die,
Divided face I'm hung with, hindside-to,
How can a peace be drawn between us, who
    Never see eye to eye?

Why, when it seems I speak straight from the heart
Most solemn thought, do you too have to speak,
Let out a horselaugh, whistle as I break
    The news to Mother that I must depart?

Moon always waxing full, barrage balloon,
Vesuvius upside down, dual rump roast,
Cave of the Winds, my Mississippi coast,
    Cyclops forever picking up and chucking stone,

Caboose, poor ass I'm saddled with from birth,
Without your act, the dirty deed I share,
How could the stuck-up spirit in me bear
    Coming back down to earth?

Creation Morning

Needing nothing, not lonely nor bored,
Why should He have let there be light?
We can only guess: a pool
Turns us so peaceful a face
That, unsettled, we take up a stone
To shatter that placidness.

Could it have been what boys know
At the rim of a new-laid sidewalk
That for empty blocks extends
Like the smooth crest of a moon
Until the tip of the chalk
Drags the hand in its wake?—

What he knows who beholds in his bride
Only her willingness,
He placing clothes on a chair,
She lying on one white side
With an imminent look?
That may have been how it was.

Who would not start growth rings
Breaking on shores of bark
At the toss of a seed like a stone,
Though not an eye look on
In that time nor in any time,
Though in the solid dark?

A Footpath near Gethsemane

for Raymond Roseliep

A Child:	Mary, Mary, wan and weary,
	What does your garden grow?
The Mother:	Tenpenny nails and Veronica's veils
	And three ruddy trees in a row.

The Atheist's Stigmata

Good Friday eve. The nail holes in my wrists
And ankles pop like bubbles. Doctor, feel
This opening in my side—put your hand there—
There—people reach out to me. Why can't I heal
Those babies? Scabs like helmets. Can't forget
By drinking—only the gradual rounding-out
Of buds in April warmth helps. Less and less
I feel that pain too human to express,
Feel my back work loose from invisible planks,
A thief again and not the Middle Man
Till next year. Father, I'd be forsaken, thanks.

Consumer's Report

They don't make things like they used to.
American proverb

At meat, or hearing you deplore
  How fast things break, my mind salutes
John Dowd, who'd bring by rolling store
Horse radish to our kitchen door
  He'd make from cream and home-ground roots.

My God. The heat of it would burn
  Holes through your beef and knock your tongue out.
Once, for a snowsuit I'd outgrown,
Came so much free stuff in return
  It smoldered down and ended flung out.

Why did he sport that look of pain
  Strangely, although his trade kept thriving?
They say the fumes get to your brain.
One day he came round with a cane
  And someone else to do the driving,

But ground right on with open eyes
  And, grinding, stared straight at his killer.
I bet theirs takes them by surprise
Though they can see, today-type guys,
  The guys who use white turnip filler.

In a Secret Field

Stealthily
The snow's soft tons

By the air
Unbearable

Accumulate.

Intermission

EPIGRAMS & EPITAPHS

Ars Poetica

The goose that laid the golden egg
Died looking up its crotch
To find out how its sphincter worked.

Would you lay well? Don't watch.

Japanese Beetles

1 *Overheard in the Louvre*

Said the Victory of Samothrace,
What winning's worth this loss of face?

2 *Apocrypha*

Great Yahweh fingered through His Bible,
Thought on it. And filed suit for libel.

3 *To Someone Who Insisted I Look Up Someone*

I rang them up while touring Timbuctoo,
Those bosom chums to whom you're known as *Who?*

4 *Sex Manual*

By the cold glow that lit my lover's eye
I could read what page eight had said to try.

5

Time is that dentist fond of sweet desserts
Who, drill in hand, says, "Stop me if this hurts."

6 *At Colonus*

Stranger: That was a sacred altar!
          You dare plant buttocks there?
Oedipus: Where gods no more set table
          May man not make his chair?

7 *To a Now-Type Poet*

Your stoned head's least whim jotted down white-hot?
Enough confusion of my own I've got.

8 *Translator*

They say he knows, who renders Old High Dutch,
His own tongue only and of it not much.

9 *Parody: Herrick*

When Vestalina's thin white hand cuts cheese
The very mice go down upon their knees.

10 *To a Young Poet*

On solemn asses fall plush sinecures,
So keep a straight face and sit tight on yours.

11 *To an Angry God*

Lend me cruel light
That, tooling over syllables I write,
I do not skim forgivingly. Not spare,
But smite.

12 *A Late Call for Armaments*

As concertgoers at soft woodwinds cough,
In time of peace, militarists sound off.

13 *Aphasia*
for C. F.

It gains on me like fat or growing bald,
This ailment of forgetting—what's it called?

14 To a Hard Core Porn-Film Leading Man

Obscure stone face, crowds cast you not a glance.
Disclose yourself—they'll know you! Drop your pants!

15 Literary Cocktail Party

Abuse pours in on all who leave the room,
Ill nature so abhors a vacuum.

16 An Editor

What do you call the taste of Peter Pitter?
A plastic spoon for straining Kitty Litter,
Whose even perforations let slip through
Never a hunk of stinking offal, true—
Just an innocuous wet-on residue.

17 On a Given Book

I slumbered with your sonnets on my bosom:
The net result of trying to peruse 'em.

18 A Note on Contributors

Writers of high renown, in *Playboy*'s hire,
    Who'd waylay men intent on spilling seed,
Remind us of Miss Prothero at the fire
    Offering the firemen something nice to read.

19 Acumen

What critic can be more acute
    Than T. P. Random-Carper
Who pokes his pencils up his chute
    And bumps-and-grinds 'em sharper?

20 An Autobiographer

With flattering mirror, while Medusa slakes
Her thirst for love, she petrifies her snakes.

21 Sappho to a Mummy Wrapped in Papyrus

Dull Pharaoh, rot in pride. Each stately line
Of your strict form lies packed in one of mine.
By priests regaled, by scarabs ravaged, sleep
Till time decide whose leftovers will keep.

22 Conformity

after Baudelaire

The Belgians won't just copy. If
    Drink is in style they'll drink to drench
Their drawers, and when they catch a syph
    They'll double-dose, to be twice French.

23 Two Lovers Proceed to Love Despite Their Sunburns

With motion slow and gingerly they place
Their outward forms, broiled bright as carapace,
Like linesmen handling bared high-tension wires
Dreading the surges of abrupt desires.

24

None but the Spirit, moving and igniting,
Deserves the credit in creative writing.

Bulsh

in memoriam: Alfred Jarry

1

Saint Bulsh bears gifts to dying paupers' hovels:
You lazy fuckers! hit these picks and shovels!

2

Bulsh in the desert prays, and camels bawl:
Head for the hills before he humps us all!

3

If visions of delight goad Bulsh, he'll beat
His breast; and if they goad him twice, his meat.

4

Hot from the hock shop Bulsh gloats. At a loss,
The devout have to skip four Stations of the Cross.

5

Before Bulsh kisses lepers' sores, his smile
He straightens, and his flattering profile.

6

With nickel poised to gong the beggar's pot
Bulsh waves the crew in for a zoom-up shot.

7   *Bulsh's motto*

Bugger the waif and screw old age unless
You're covered on prime time by CBS.

8

When Bulsh clears his throat to preach, falls a great hush,
The whole cathedral emptied in one flush.

9

Why does Bulsh laugh like some bad child of Belloc's?
He's won first grabs at Saint Swinessa's relics.

10

Suffer our little Brother Lark to come,
Leers Bulsh, with open cookbook under thumb.

11

For penance, buster, smell me breaking wind!—
Lately in Bulsh's parish none has sinned.

12

Plump girls stay pasted fast to Bulsh's slat,
Old bony ones he shrives in no time flat.

13

When grave Bulsh counsels girls about to be brides,
In the dim booth he hoots and holds his sides.

14

Wise nuns at Mass keep bulldogs in their pew
Lest Bulsh's fingers play the Wandering Jew.

15

Young matrons pray, *Saint Bulsh, man, get me pregnant!*
(His device: testicles, with penis regnant.)

16   *Bulsh, hearing St. Matthew on publicans and sinners*

I shouldn't bitch, I'm just one of the sheep,
But, Jesus Christ! the company you keep!

17

On old Skull Hill, Bulsh hollered up the Cross:
Want me to spell you for a minute, boss?

18

What? Me rat on our Savior? Up your ass!
That'll be FORTY dracks, plus lunch and gas.

19

Bulsh spies the tired step of the old Pope.
Within his breast quickens a certain hope.

20

Bulsh on the crapper thinks: What could be sweeter
Than squatter's access to the throne of Peter?

21   *Bulsh to the nuns*

Go buzz off, sisters, no more hosts to bake.
I fed one to a nigger by mistake.

22   *Satan on the mountaintop*

Why in Hell not adore me, Bulsh, my pretty?
You do it to me, I'll take Jersey City.

23   *Satan again*

I'll net the big trout yet. One of my ploys
Is dangling Bulsh pink wriggling altar boys.

24

Hooker, her festered lips sublime with ooze,
Made Bulsh an offer too good to refuse.

25   *Bulsh's* Carpe Diem

Almighty God's a patient elevator.
Drink and fuck now, and be assumpted later.

26

When Bulsh found out he hadn't long to live
He fell to giving God more to forgive.

27   *Satan again*

What? Bulsh given extreme unction? Bless it! Foiled!
Slippery as eels he is. And always oiled.

28   *Bulsh lays a fat one*

High noon grows ominous, hard gravemounds heave
And, caught off balance, Doubting Toms believe.

29

On Resurrection morn it sore surprised
Bulsh to stand up and go unrecognized.

Last Lines

1 *For a Postal Clerk*

Here lies wrapped up tight in sod
Henry Harkins c/o God.
On the day of Resurrection
May be opened for inspection.

2 *For a Man Overboard*

Once born, once married, once self-drowned,
I take this wave to be my mound.
One tear, dry reader, will suffice:
Nothing once done would I do twice.

3 *From the Greek Anthology*

On miserable Nearchos' bones lie lightly, earth,
That the dogs may dig him up, for what he's worth.

4

Here lies a girl whose beauty made Time stay.
Shovel earth in. We haven't got all day.

5 *For a Teutonic Scholar*

One night Professor Kleit, mere dust and bone,
Rose to correct the deathdate on his stone
And added, with habitual precision,
A finely chiseled footnote of derision.

6 *For an Exotic Dancer*

She'd met the premiums. One last revealing
Would feed her kid. Slowly undoing feeling
Like a tied string, she let fall all beneath.
Drums bumped. Old Boneyard whistled through cracked teeth.

Last Lines for Athletes

1

Full-nelsoned in earth's arms, the Crusher sleeps,
Whom no one living ever pinned for keeps.

2

Stilled in his corner, Ahmed takes the count.
He won't get up again for any amount.

3

Ron fades back and, his options in decline,
Is brought down on the two-yard-under line.

4

Here lies Top Seed, who battered frisky balls
Thousands of times at top speed off brick walls
To hard-sell TV viewers on a brand
Difficult to destroy and vacuum-canned.
A swinging doubles star, he freely came
With any old kind of partner you could name—
Woman or babe; transvestite, man, or beast;
Any warm body adequately greased—
Only to make one point in lying here:
At breaking balls, Death's service has no peer.

Flesh Is Grass

1

A new-laid lawn emits hand-lettered cries:
KEEP OFF ME AND ONE DAY I'LL LET *YOU* RISE.

2

Dumb sods, we feel our roots lift loose before
The slow chomp of some patient herbivore,

Or, spun to death, revolve through Hades' shades
Writhing inside a wind like mower blades.

The Devil's Advice to Poets

Molt that skin! lift that face!—you'll go far.
Grow like Proteus yet more bizarre.
   In perpetual throes
   Majors metamorphose—
Only minors remain who they are.

To the One-Eyed Poets

Creeley, Penn Warren, and James Seay,
Did sight hold sway, and mind,
The likes of you might well be kings
In this country of the blind.

IV

1972–1977

Last Child

for Daniel

Small vampire, gorger at your mother's teat,
Dubious claim I didn't know I'd staked,
Like boomerangs your cries reverberate
Till roused half-blind, I bear you to be slaked,
Your step-and-fetch-it pimp.
                              Fat lot you care
If meadows fall before your trash-attack,
Streams go to ruin, waste be laid to air.
Will yours be that last straw that breaks earth's back?

Your fingers writhe: inane anemones
A decent ocean ought to starve. Instead
I hold you, I make tries at a caress.
You should not be. I cannot wish you dead.

Mining Town

Sheds for machines that lower tons of men
Hug dirt for dear life. Clapboard houses lose
Gray clapboards the way a dying oak sheds bark.
One house they tell of plunged
Nose-down into a shaft last year with cries
Of sleepers waking, falling.

Like boys in sneakers testing limber ice,
Gas stations growing bold now inch up near.
Who recollects that Kitchen Kounter World
Straddles Pit One? Dull coaloil-colored clouds
Graze to the west.

Born in this town, you learn to sleep on edge,
Always on edge, to grow up like a tree
Locked to the wind's sharp angle. When fear tells
It tells out of the corner of an eye,
A rickety house balancing in uncertainty.

Onan's Soliloquy

She'll none of me? Like Hell. She's mine alone.
Self-ordained priest, I elevate my bone;
Behind slammed lids, behold her toothsome bust
Projected wobbling on a screen of dust;
Skim her clitoris's pert dot of braille,
Led by a German shepherd round her tail;
Fumble her dim unconscionable tits,
Darkness all mine for lover. And I its.

Emily Dickinson in Southern California

1

I called one day – on Eden's strand
But did not find her – Home –
Surfboarders triumphed in – in Waves –
Archangels of the Foam –

I walked a pace – I tripped across
Browned couples – in cahoots –
No more than Tides need shells to fill
Did they need – bathing suits –

From low boughs – that the Sun kist – hung
A Fruit to taste – at will –
October rustled but – Mankind
Seemed elsewhere gone – to Fall –

2

The Tour Boat hurtles – Newport Bay –
Till I go by – in flood –
An Island – Jimmy Cagney won –
One night – at high card stud –

And genuflecting to a Breeze –
White-bosomed Schooners – dodge –
Obeisant as Gondolas
Before a passing Doge –

I spy the House – that King Gillette
Whom Whiskers – had enthroned –
Built Wings so wide – they quite sliced off
His nextdoor Brother's – sun –

And prickling as it chills – the Bay
Beholds a Full Moon rise
That – squeezing earthward through a Lens
Of Smog – Immensifies –

3

There is a habitude – of Sound –
Intrinsic – to the Skull –
To keep a Measure stalking – though
Pendulums stand still –

How Oversized the fallen Hush –
It takes a whittling Ear
To shave it to a Point – and push
Hard through – till One – unhear –

4

When Hopelessness – moved in with me –
He brought a ball of Twine
And wrapped it three times – round my heart –
To keep my heart – in line –

And every time my heart – thrashed up –
He'd jerk back till – each Valve
Drew shut and – reined there – flittering –
I'd watch the Light – dissolve –

And then he'd whisper – me in Hand –
"Dear little sister – how
Can you wish other – than this Earth
And all its Goods?" – And now –

Content to peck – his bitter Grits –
It sits here – being His –
And would no longer dream – to Soar –
For all the Sky – there is –

5

I took my Spirit – for a walk –
A scabbed Thing – and a scaled –
Tongued with the flicker of a Snake
And Alligator-tailed –

Its Belly – grated raw the Ground –
Its mailed Feet marched in rows –
Down to the thick black Lily pond
I drove it – it nosed ooze –

And – thirsting – lunged as some Toad would –
And bubbled out of sight –
The wasted Sun sat down – I stood –
The Dark leapt bolt upright –

And held me – clenched – I couldn't breathe
One Pulsebeat more – when out
That Beast broke! Like a Blizzard banked –
White Lilies wreathed its Snout –

6

The Storm came home too blind to stand –
He thwacked down Oaks like chairs –
Shattered a Lake and – in the dark –
Head over heels downstairs
Rolled – and up grumbling on his knees
Made nine white tries to scratch
Against Walls – that kept billowing –
The strict head of his Match –

7

I'm loath to tolerate a Sky
That will not stand for Storm –
As Ceiling were to militate
Against Sound in its Room –

The Concord orchard Macintosh –
Wart-cheeked and bubble-chinned –
Has freckles like an Aunt you'd trust
And handclasp – like a Friend –

But gazing at the Fresno – Grape –
Of sleek perfectioned Jaw –
I fear the Planet should gape wide –
Did One discern its Flaw –

8

I bore Hope's candle farthest West –
And now – obliged to halt –
Hear Asia's rumor of Despair
Beyond a wall of Salt –

Schizophrenic Girl

Having crept out this far,
So close your breath casts moisture on the pane,
Your eyes blank lenses opening part way
To the dead moonmoth fixed with pins of rain,
Why do you hover here,
A swimmer not quite surfaced, inches down,
Fluttering water, making up her mind
To breathe, or drown?

All the fall long, earth deepening its slant
Back from the level sun, you wouldn't quit
That straitbacked chair they'd dress you in. You'd sit,
Petrified fire, casting your frozen glare,
Not swallowing, refusing to concede
There are such things as spoons. And so they'd feed
You through a vein
Cracked open like a lake they'd icefish in—
Can no one goad
You forth into the unsteady hearthlight of the sane?

Already, yawning child
At some dull drawn-out adult affair,
You whimper for permission to retire
To your right room where black
T-squares of shadows lie, vacuity
A sheet drawn halfway back.

If you'd just cry. Involved
Around some fixed point we can't see, you whirl
In a perpetual free-fall.
Come forth. We cannot stand
To see turned into stone what had been hand,
What had been mind smoothed to a bright steel ball.

Crawfish

after Apollinaire

Uncertainty O my secret joy
To make tracks you and I
Must turn tail like the craw
And withdraw and withdraw

Evening Tide

Darkness invades the shallows of the street.
A tricycle left outdoors starts nodding and bobbing.

On its recliner by dusk set afloat
Father's head lolls, its dome of beer half-emptied.

Under the parked car in the driveway, shadows seep.
From somewhere the cry of a child protesting bed
Comes blundering in again and again, a stick of driftwood.

Celebrations After the Death of John Brennan

1

What do they praise, those friends of his who leap
Into a frenzied joy since Brennan died
By his own rifle in his mother's house
Along a rock road on a mountainside?
Do they bring gong and incense, do they stage
Some egocentric homemade Buddhist Mass?

Word stops me as I'm climbing Medford Hill,
Poor East Coast Rocky, ice still in its grass.
I hold on to a railing, dragging steps
Up stepping-planks. Two lines he'd written stare:
Why is it *celebrations often seem*
contrived as war?

2

Churned by the wind, the iceberg of his death
Slowly revolves, a huge stage without act.
A seat bangs like a gunshot—pushbrooms sweep
Litter of paper: poems, scribbled chords
For his guitar. Days earlier he'd climbed
To East Hall, where the litterati live,
And had me get a load of one last song.
Could I have turned him from his blackout phase?
Could anyone? For many must have sensed
A furious desperation in his gaiety.
Chance not to grieve dissolving moons—
An ashen grin of craters on the wane
Emerges and submerges through white waves.

3

Forever looking freshly tumbled out
Of a haystack he'd shacked up in, cockeyed grin

Disarming as a swift kick to the chin,
He had a way that put pretense to rout.
That was one hell of an opening
Pedagogue-student conference!—
Cracking rot-gut red in his dorm pad
Till we basked in dippy glows,
Reading aloud his latest hundred poems:
Fragments of mirror ranged along a strand
For sun to rise on, overflow, expose.

4

Teachers and shrinks had pestered him to vow
He'd tread in straight lines—John the circler-by
And lazy wheeler! *Does your infinity*
start sooner than mine? How could he die
From no more than a quarrel with a friend
Or lovers' falling-out?
                          Yet he had backpacked
Death telescoped, ready, a hiker's metal cup
Along his mountain path. One day he'd drink.
He'd seen it clear: each poem
A last note scribbled in a hand that shook
I'd been too blind to read. This aftermath
Of snow betrays the walk.

5

Dissolved, those fugitive songs
Blown out of mind: breath from a halted lung—
As though a burst of rain had stricken away
Bright beaded webs the dew had barely strung.

6

Home from his Sligo ramble, skipped sleep nights
Tooling his pen-and-inks, photographs, words.
Self-published his tombstone

In that one cryptic book
And like Huck Finn attended his own rites.

I break it open. Now its message stares,
Plain, that back then had seemed half rained away.
His lens had gorged on thorns, worn timbers, chains,
A ruined abbey, stonework walls a loss
Where one surviving gunslot window yields
A foot-wide view of a constricted cross,
Black children peering through an iron gate—
columbines grow well in boulderfields.

7

Gowned as a clown with greasepaint tears drawn on,
John wraps stunned Seymour Simches six times round
With monkey rope,
Trusses himself up too,
Pratfalls.
The floor implodes. And everyone drops through.

I'd not aspire to be your father, John.
I meant only to copyread your words.
Hard enough now—four blood sons of my own
Trussing me too
In dried umbilical cords.

8

"Well, most of me's still here," my old man said
After the surgeon pared him, hospitaled,
Needing no son's swordthrust where three roads meet:
Eighty-eight, yet guileless as a child,
Still hanging on. John gone. Which one is wise,
A young man worn with age or a wizened boy?
To cling to life with fingerless right hand
Or, with a twitch of a finger, blow it away?

9

Flown from your Rockies, John, did you find home,
Second home on the gaunt cliffs of Moher
Whose face held hide-outs from the Black and Tans,
Men perched in grottoes, cawing out to sea?
Stuck in those crags, did you defy the gale,
Dreaming, a scrap of turfgrass in your fist,
Your long look swooping in an arc to trace
The coastline of a gull?

10

Shank end of spring. A night held in his name.
A full throng waxes. Thin forsythia
Of Medford thrusts indifferent sprigs again.
No prayers, no introductions, no plan,
Yet each knows when to rise and speak in turn
Or do a simple dance, sing, or read lines,
When to join arms, to circle, to return.
Nothing's decreed and yet all present know
The clockstroke when the celebration ends.
The wine stands lower in its gallon jug,
The night grows warm, reluctant to grow late.
It is John Brennan not John Brennan's death
We celebrate.

Goblet

from Hugo von Hofmannsthal

Goblet in hand, she strode to him,
Her small chin level with its rim,
So light her stride and she so skilled
At fetching, not a drop she spilled.

Steady as hers was his own hand
That drew his ripple-muscled colt
Shuddering to an abrupt halt
With a casual gesture of command—

And yet as he stretched forth his hand
Almost to hers and would take hold,
The goblet seemed too huge to take.
Because the two of them so shook
Neither could find the other's hand.
Over the ground the dark wine rolled.

Dirty English Potatoes

Baildon, West Yorkshire

Steam-cleaned, so groundless you'd believe
  Them exhaled from some passing cloud,
The Idahoes and Maines arrive
  Same-sized, tied in their plastic shroud.

Their British kindred, unconfined,
  Differ in breeding, taste, and size.
They come with stones you mustn't mind.
  You have to dredge their claypit eyes.

Their brows look wrinkled with unease
  Like chilblain-sufferers in March.
No sanitized machines are these
  For changing sunlight into starch—

Yet the new world's impatient taint
  Sticks to my bones. I can't resist
Cursing my mucked-up sink. I want
  Unreal meals risen from sheer mist.

No Neutral Stone

Starved sod, those grayish neutral tones, and ashen
  Leaves at the numb pond's edge—does frost hold sway
  Over all nature only to display
The dregs of young Tom Hardy's summer passion?

"Bright star!" breathes Keats, and Venus thus invoked
  Scrapes dog dung from her soles and comes indoors.
  Planets may want no part in human wars,
Yet serve, by poet conscript-sergeants yoked.

Write not "I love," says Eliot. Name an ocean.
  Feelings pre-empt dull matter, whose debris
  Sprawls formless till some passing poet—whee!—
Hoists an electromagnet of emotion

And lets it fall to wallow in scrap steel.
  Clattering, spare parts leap in droves to kiss
  His charming plate. He shifts gears—the whole mess
Dangles aloft: precisely what he'd feel

Frozen in one triumphant junkyard-sweep,
  Oddly assorted as a homemade car
  Whose backfire draws your stare—spectacular!
Meanwhile, in the rejected world's trash heap,

Some rusting wheel or gearshift lever sighs,
  Complaining to the rain's incessant pelt:
  What? Am I not what Hardy must have felt,
Alone, after Tryphena slammed her thighs?

Aunt Rectita's Good Friday

Plate-scraping at her sink, she consecrates
To Christ her Lord the misery in her legs.
Tinges of spring engage the bulbous land.
Packets of dyestuff wait for Easter eggs.

Frail-boned, stooped low as she, forsythia
In its decreptitude yet ventures flowers.
How can He die and how dare life go on?
A beer truck desecrates God's passionate hours.

He died for those who do not give a damn.
Brooding on sorrowful mysteries, she shoves
Into its clean white forehead-fat the ham's
Thorn crown of cloves.

Intermission

FOR CHILDREN

King Tut

King Tut
Crossed over the Nile
On stepping stones
Of crocodile.

King Tut!
His mother said,
Come here this minute!
You'll get wet feet.
King Tut is dead

And now King Tut
Tight as a nut
Keeps his big fat Mummy shut.

King Tut,
Tut, tut.

Where Will We Run To

Where will we run to
When the moon's
Polluted in her turn
And the sun sits
With its wheels blocked
In the used star lot?

Snowflake Soufflé

Snowflake soufflé
Snowflake soufflé
Makes a lip-smacking lunch
On an ice-cold day!

You take seven snowflakes,
You break seven eggs,
And you stir it seven times
With your two hind legs.

Bake it in an igloo,
Throw it on a plate,
And you slice off a slice
With a rusty ice-skate.

Vulture

The vulture's very like a sack
    Set down and left there drooping.
His crooked neck and creaky back
    Look badly bent from stooping
Down to the ground to eat dead cows
    So they won't go to waste
Thus making up in usefulness
    For what he lacks in taste.

Mother's Nerves

My mother said, "If just once more
I hear you slam that old screen door,
I'll tear out my hair! I'll dive in the stove!"
I gave it a bang and in she dove.

Should All of This Come True

If combs could brush their teeth,
If a needle's eye shed tears,
If bottles craned their necks,
If corn pricked up its ears,

If triangles held their sides
And laughed, if down the street
A mile like a millipede
Ran by on wavy feet,

If cans of laundry lye
Declared they tell no fibs,
If baked potatoes dug
Umbrellas in the ribs,

If sheets of rain were starched,
If a brook, with mutterings,
Rolled over in its bed
With a deep creek of springs,

Should all of this come true
And all time were to pass,
Then you could slice a piece of cheese
With any blade of grass.

Two Doorbells

Two doorbells glowered out at me
With buttons big and bright.
Which one to push? Was it the left
Or the right one that was right?

I plucked up courage, pushed the right,
I pushed it good and strong—
An angry eagle came. Good night!
I must have rung dead wrong!

He shrieked, "I've flown down one whole flight
Of stairs, you runt! Pray tell,
What makes you think you've got a right
To wrong me and my bell?"

He slammed the door so hard it left
My glasses with no glass.
Well, I gave the left-hand bell a press—
Right soon, a braying ass,

A rhino with his rump on wrong,
A tribe of owls that sang
An odd, foul-sounding sort of song,
A red orang-utang,

A mummy coming all unwrapped
And a huge blue shark replied.
The shark, his jawbones open, snapped:
"Why don't you step inside?"

I turned toes right around and left,
Which didn't take me long.
I'd got the number right, all right,
But that street was downright wrong.

A Visit to the Gingerbread House

"Why, sit down!" (So I let myself settle
In a fudge chair.) "I'll put on the kettle,"
    Purred the Witch. "Here, just try
    Some delicious toad pie
And a cup of hot Hansel and Gretel!"

Crocodile

The Crocodile's a social sort:
In bumpy green apparel
Crocs paddle round their jungle pool
Like pickles in a barrel.

The Crocodile can smile with style
And chuckle kindly, too.
Oh, they're the friendliest of beasts—
In fact, they're fond of *you!*

Lion

Who bounded headfirst from the Ark?
    Whose roar's a hurricane?
Who shakes whole jungles in the dark
    With all his might and mane?

Lion. That's who adores to roar
    And when you're with a Lion
The nearest house that has a door
    Is good to keep an eye on.

To a Forgetful Wishing Well

All summer long, your round stone eardrum held
Wishes I whispered down you. None came true.
Didn't they make one ripple in your mind?
I'd even wished a silver pail for you.

Brats

1

John while swimming in the ocean
Rubbed sharks' backs with suntan lotion.
Now those sharks have skin of bronze
In their bellies—namely, John's.

2

Stealing eggs, Fritz ran afoul
Of an angry great horned owl.
Now she has him—what a catch!—
Seeing if his head will hatch.

3

Doris Drummond sneaked a look
In a locked and cobwebbed book,
Found some secret words you said
That could summon up the dead.
Sad to say, the dead she summoned
Had it in for Doris Drummond.

4

Vince released a jar of vermin
During Mister Drowser's sermon
On how cheerfulness is catching.
Soon the whole next pew was scratching.

5

At the market Philbert Spicer
Peered into the cold-cut slicer—
Whiz! the wicked slicer sped
Back and forth across his head
Quickly shaving—what a shock!—
Fifty chips off Phil's old block,
Stopping just above the eyebrows.
Phil's not one of them there highbrows.

V
1978–1984

Hangover Mass

Of all sins of the flesh, that reprobate
  My father had but one, and it had class:
To sip tea of a Sunday till so late
  We'd barely make it up to Drunkards' Mass.

After a sermon on the wiles of booze,
  The bread and wine transformed with decent haste,
Quickly the priest would drive us forth to graze
  Where among churchyard flocks I'd get a taste

Of chronic loneliness. Red-rimmed of eye,
  Quaking of hand, old men my old man knew
Would congregate to help bad time go by:
  Stout Denny Casey, gaunt Dan Donahue

Who'd mention girls with withering contempt,
  Each man long gone past hope to meet his match
Unless in what he drank all night, or dreamt.
  Each knee I stared at cried out for a patch.

A sealed half-pint, I'd stand there keeping mum
  Till, bored to death, I'd throw a fit of shakes.
Then with relief we'd both go stepping home
  Over sidewalk cracks' imaginary snakes.

One-Night Homecoming

Opening the door, he grasps my suitcase handle,
But can't quite lift it. Breathes hard, mounting stairs.
She doesn't notice yolk stuck to the dishes,
Nailheads arising from the kitchen chairs.

Where are the kids? In school. *You didn't bring them?*
I'll be your kid, I say, but can't compete
With her persistent needling iteration
That hurts without intending to, like sleet.

From childhood's bed I follow in the ceiling
The latest progress of each crack I know,
But still the general cave-in hangs suspended,
Its capillary action running slow,

And the huge roof I used to think unchanging
Gives with each wind. It's my turn now to fall
Over strewn blocks, stuffed animals on staircases,
My turn to read the writing crayoned on the wall.

October

Flat-tired, the year sets out red roadside flares.
  A football's olive in a casual toss
  Ovals its chain of overthrows across
Its briskly stirred martini. But the air's

As of two minds: to thunder or forgive?
  Clouds hold their fire. The parching widow's-bless
  Purses weak lips. Trees' signals of distress
Turn more flamboyantly demonstrative.

Were we two stout perennials at heart
  Who knows what light we'd make of time's abuse.
  Sleep near me. Be a tough nut to work loose
Before harsh hoarfrost wrenches us apart.

Joshua

Earth stopped. The Holy City hit a mountain
As a tray of dishes meets a swinging door.
Oceans lunged to converge, one with another.
He who had called that halt stood bemused there.

Who would have thought a simple invocation . . . ?
As brazen leaves, troops fell. His walking stick
Tapped as he limped across a foiled battalion.
Sun and moon hung stone still, their axles stuck.

No cricket sprang from upright walls of grass.
Clouds swung in bunches, wingless. Who could look
Long on so high a carnage: all creation
Crushed like a sprig of heather in a book?

Futile to wail, wear sackcloth, tear his tongue out—
How could he feel commensurate remorse?
At last the sun, God resting noncommittal,
Rose in confusion and resumed its course.

Old Men Pitching Horseshoes

Back in a yard where ringers groove a ditch,
These four in shirtsleeves congregate to pitch
Dirt-burnished iron. With appraising eye,
One sizes up a peg, hoists and lets fly—
A clang resounds as though a smith had struck
Fire from a forge. His first blow, out of luck,
Rattles in circles. Hitching up his face,
He swings, and weight once more inhabits space,
Tumbles as gently as a new-laid egg.
Extended iron arms surround their peg
Like one come home to greet a long-lost brother.
Shouts from one outpost. Mutters from the other.

Now changing sides, each withered pitcher moves
As his considered dignity behooves
Down the worn path of earth where August flies
And sheaves of air in warm distortions rise,
To stand ground, fling, kick dust with all the force
Of shoes still hammered to a living horse.

Similes

1

As fallen snow, allowed to take firm hold
   While all inside draw solace from the fire,
Revolving brandy in balloons of gold,
   No shoveler at the doorbell seeking hire,
Exerts its weight in silence, and slow rain
   Seals and defines the content of each drift,
So our misunderstanding, settling in,
   Hardened to ice impossible to lift.

2

Gladly I do without you. At my hands
   Go catch your death of absence. Yet my mood's
   As one's who flees society for woods
While, obstinate, the world he'd quit withstands
The downfall he so yearns for, but exudes
   Top popsong hits, diurnal tax demands.
   And he grown gaunt from guarding Krugerrands,
Supping on crow and parched survival foods.

3

As killers who'd accelerate decay,
   Goading the earth, who takes her own sweet time,
   Pour on an upturned face a cloud of lime,
Their hopes misplaced in worms they drive away,
So you and I who meet again by chance,
   Thinking love's lips disbanded under proud
   Recriminations, hear them cry aloud
Our ancient pet names, turned state's evidence.

Ool About to Proclaim a Parable

Plato thought nature but a spume that plays
Upon a ghostly paradigm of things . . .

Yeats

One Flash of it within the Tavern caught
Better than in the Temple lost outright.

FitzGerald's Khayyám

Pounded the bar. In Mickey's Liffeyside
All but the muted TV set fell still.
Hands over shuffleboard hung petrified
While, hoisting high and struggling not to spill

His foam-domed glass, Ool bellowed: "See this fizz?"—
Siddown, somebody yelled, *you damned old souse—*
"The human race, the head on draft beer is!"—
A low guffaw loped houndlike round the house.

"But what's below the suds line? What's he called
That rides us suckers on his golden breast,
Trickling up bubbles?"—*Ool,* somebody bawled,
Gas with your ass, man, give your mouth a rest.

Fluorescent lightning prowled each outraged face.
The pitcher shuddering in his fist, Ool poured
A second glass, blew off the human race,
And drank deep of the fullness of the Lord.

To Dorothy on Her Exclusion
from the *Guinness Book of World Records*

Not being Breedlove, whose immortal skid
Bore him for six charmed miles on screeching brakes;
Not having whacked from Mieres to Madrid
The longest-running hoop; at ducks and drakes
The type whose stone drowns in a couple of skips
Even if pittypats be counted plinkers;
Smashing of face, but having launched no ships;
Not of a kidney with beer's foremost drinkers;

Fewer the namesakes that display your brand
Than Prout has little protons—yet you win
The world with just a peerless laugh. I stand
Stricken amazed: you merely settle chin
Into a casual fixture of your hand
And a uniqueness is, that hasn't been.

At the Last Rites for Two Hotrodders

Sheeted in steel, embedded face to face,
They idle now in feelingless embrace,
The only ones at last who had the nerve
To meet head-on, not chicken out and swerve.

Inseparable, in one closed car they roll
Down the stoned aisle and on out to a hole,
Wheeled by the losers: six of fledgling beard,
Black-jacketed and glum, who also steered
Toward absolute success with total pride,
But, inches from it, felt, and turned aside.

Flitting Flies

They come. No sooner do I lift
Eyelids on day than out they drift:
Invaders dim as blobs of rain
Or spaceships made of cellophane.

Alert for signs of bad intent,
I watch. So far, benevolent.
What earthly purpose can they serve,
These vermin of the optic nerve?

Between my retina and light
They blur each page I read or write,
Squiggling their plumes, and slowly trace
Amorphous progresses through space.

When in the heat of puberty
These vague May flies first rose in me,
I thought my hangdog soul abhorred
In the fierce eyeball of the Lord—

Took them for Limbo's brats let loose
To strike me blind for self-abuse
And in each ectoplasmic blot
Beheld some wraith I'd half begot.

Near summer's climax now, I know
That in their escort I must go
To walk my last mile, let go free
By jailors ignorant of me.

At least, from peering out through cells
I know that blindness to what dwells

Too far beyond or swarms too near
Is my best hope of seeing clear,

No longer certain there can be
Ideal fish of porphyry
Nor indiscriminately fond
Of lurkers deep in my own pond.

The Death of Professor Backwards

slain January 29, 1976

Three hot-eyed kids hard on a fix's heels,
Enraged at the cash he had, few bills and small,
Did in James Edmondson, famed vaudeville's
Professor Backwards. Three slugs through the skull
Closed his great act: the Gettysburg Address
About he'd switch and back-to-front deliver.
Transposed perfectly them at back hurl he'd
Out called crowd the in hecklers any whatever.

More than clashed glass in Vegas clubs fell still
That night his heart backpaddled to a stop:
Unheard lay songs that once with dazzling skill
His brainpan's funhouse mirror used to flop.
A listening Sennett, applause his to command,
Why had it to be him, so lean of purse,
Felled like a dog in an alley when his blind
Fate shot back like a truck parked in reverse
To hurl him backwards, trailing gory clouds?

The world will little note and long forget
How any watcher in whole spellbound crowds
Would light the wrong end of a cigarette.

You Touch Me

You touch me.
  One by one
In each cell of my body
  A hearth comes on.

On the Proposed Seizure of Twelve Graves in a Colonial Cemetery

Word rustles round the burying-ground
Down path and pineconed byway.
The Commonwealth craves twelve heroes' graves
For a turn-lane in its highway.

Town meeting night, debate is slight:
Defenders of tradition
Twitter and cheep, too few to keep
The dead from fresh perdition.

With white-hot gaze emitting rays
Observes Selectman Earnwright,
"Some stupid corpse just wastes and warps
Where traffic needs to turn right!"

Embattled still within his hill,
One farmer loosed a snicker.
"When once ten redcoats dogged my arse,
I did not light out quicker

"Than when in a foss our scraps they'll toss
Therein to blend and nuzzle
Till God's last trump lift skull and rump,
One risen Chinese puzzle!

"Late yesterday as I listening lay
And the sweet rain kindly seeping,
I would have sworn I heard Gabe's horn—
'Twas but rush-hour's beeping.

"Ah, on my life, old Marth my wife
Will soon regret I chose her

When through our bosom-bones protrude
Posterity's bulldozer."

Rose a voice in wrath from under the path:
"Why skulk we in this cavern?
Come, lads, to arms!—as once we formed
One morn at good Fitch Tavern!

"Are we mild milksops nowadays?
Do not we still resemble
The men we were, for all Time's wear?
Repair your bones! Assemble!"

But the first wraith gave a scornful laugh.
"With muskets long outmoded?
We'd stuff the crows like thrown-down grain
Ere our poor barrels we'd loaded.

"For we dead," mused Seth, "but squander breath
On current ears. 'Tis plain
They'd amputate Christ's outstretched arms
To make a right-turn lane."

Fall Song

after Verlaine

Low notes drawn long,
Fall's fiddlesong
  Makes moan,
Lets heart loll
In its dull
  Monotone.

Weak from shock
While the clock
  Strikes, I lie.
Memories raise
Olden days
  And I cry.

I go away
Any old way
  Ill winds drive:
Here, there—off
Like a leaf
  Once alive.

A Beardsley Moment

Adoze upon her vast aplomb,
  The tittering-stock of palace mice,
Lulled by the ticking of her bombe
  Of deliquescent orange ice,

Victoria forgets to reign:
  From slackening hand crochet-hook falls
Oblivious, though snails design
  Priapic doodads down the walls,

Though Dryads merge and Mignonette,
  Venereal hair a lilac bruise
Beneath drawers of lace fishing-net,
  Discards—plip, plop!—her swansdown shoes

In bed, a plate. A satyr carves.
  Off in a corner, veiled from scorn,
Sly hoptoads with the heads of dwarves
  Fall to a whimpering unicorn,

Its wide eyes Albert's as a child.
  Now centaurs, pearl-rope-draped, in drag,
Bear off the head of Oscar Wilde
  To Paris in a Gladstone bag.

Not Marble

When one twin tower of the Board of Trade
  Works like a domino its mate's collapse,
  These potent lines might stick around, perhaps;
Or come to mind in some dim Everglade
Should one survivor still have tongue to move,
  Stealing a moment from his fishing-hook
  To mutter what he read once in some book
To another half-starved victim whom he love.

But what if doom's no circus of MacLeish?
  Suppose no black pall drops, and none but flies
Settle upon my words—then PhDish
  Plodders alone may engineer your rise
And once more, through a frame of microfiche,
  From footnotes' knotholes stare your peerless eyes.

Epiphany

Flat on my belly, sprawled at the head of the stairs,
I shuffled junk mail on the kitchen floor.
Bills, begs, and bull.
      A bolt of sunlight writhed—
Leaped—stung me in the lenses unawares.

For days I'd gone on trudging, too far dulled
To take mere things in. Floored now, freed from airs
Of uprightness, I raised astounded eyes
To how they joined—the legs and rungs of chairs.

Envoi

Go, slothful book. Just go.
Ten years slopping around the house in your sock-feet
Sucking up to a looking-glass
Rehearsing your face. Why
Don't you get a job?

Sing for the one who will care
Should words with a rhythm align.
Sing, yet not contrive
Clear sense to rob.

Sing in the loosening hands
Of lovers who may read late
While embers anguish underneath a grate.
Sing as your weight, abandoned then,
Crash-lands.

Notes

For a reader who might care to trace the progress of my work, or its deterioration, I have sorted these poems into five sections; then, within each section, arranged things from early to late, following the order in which they first appeared. In between these five acts, each section called an *Intermission* offers light refreshment. Like each act, each intermission also follows a chronology—one that begins as early as 1955 and ends as late as 1984, since it displays a kind of verse I have been writing off and on all this while. Except for sections I and II, each section of the book, and each intermission, contains some work not collected before.

ON CERTAIN POEMS

"Ant Trap" makes allusion to W. T. Scott's poem "The U.S. Sailor with the Japanese Skull."

"The Atheist's Stigmata" is not pure fiction. In 1970 the Associated Press reported the plight of a Viennese atheist on whose body the stigmatic wounds faithfully appeared every Good Friday.

"Celebrations After the Death of John Brennan" pays tribute to the most flamboyantly promising young poet I have known. John Michael Brennan was born in Denver in 1950 and died of a self-inflicted gunshot wound in Denver in February 1973. He had been a student at Tufts, in Medford, Massachusetts, where I had been his teacher and at times his student. About a year before his death, Brennan had dropped out of college to travel alone through England and Ireland. Home again in Denver in the summer of 1972, he self-published his only book, *Air is,* a collection of poems, drawings, and photographs he had taken on his journey. In my poem, italics indicate quotations from that book. Brennan returned to Tufts in the fall and enrolled in the College Within, an experimental program whose director was Seymour Simches. On April 25, 1973, an evening at the College Within was devoted to Brennan's memory.

"Goblet," a version of Hofmannsthal's "Die Bieden" ("The Two of Them"), was written in friendly competition with Robert Bly. He had challenged poets who write in meter and rime to set him poems he could not translate better into open forms. Our two attempts appeared side by side in *Counter/Measures* Three (1974).

"No Neutral Stone" refers to Thomas Hardy's early lyric "Neutral Tones." Some think Hardy depicts the aftermath of his unsuccessful courtship of his cousin Tryphena Sparks.

"To Dorothy on Her Exclusion from the *Guinness Book of World Records*" refers to a few facts given in that standard work of reference. According to Guinness, the physicist Prout claimed to have named the proton after himself. If his claim prevails, then evidently Prout holds a world's record for having the most objects in the universe bear his name.

Other Titles in the Contemporary Poetry Series